TOP PRIORITY

Building an Evangelistic Church

TOP PRIORITY

Building an Evangelistic Church

John Caldwell

 COLLEGE PRESS
PUBLISHING COMPANY
Joplin, Missouri

Library of Congress Cataloging-in-Publication Data

Caldwell, John, 1944–
    Top priority: building an evangelistic church / John Caldwell.
        p.   cm.
    ISBN 0-89900-739-2 (pbk.)
    1. Evangelistic work.   2. Witness bearing (Christianity).
3. Pastoral theology.   I. Title.
BV3793.C33 1995
269'.2–dc20   95-17518
                                                          CIP

Dedicated to

DON DEWELT & WOODROW PHILLIPS

whose classroom teaching and personal example
sparked my enthusiasm for ministry and evangelism.
Only eternity will reveal the extent of their
influence in motivating others to reach the lost for Christ.

TABLE OF CONTENTS

ACKNOWLEDGMENTS

Ever since I really got serious about my Christian life, when I was a sophomore pre-med student at Southwest Missouri State University in Springfield, Missouri, I have had the conviction that the primary purpose of the church is evangelism. That conviction was fueled in part by Jack Martin, the preacher of my home church at the time. He personally discipled me, modeled evangelism for me, and took me along with him on several evangelistic calls.

My first year at Ozark Bible College (now Ozark Christian College), my conviction as to the primacy of evangelism was further encouraged by both the teaching and example of several godly professors. However, the two who most influenced my life were Don DeWelt and Woodrow Phillips. How I thank God for these two men, whose heart for evangelism was obvious both in the classroom and in the world. It was my privilege to observe both men numerous times as they lovingly shared their faith with the lost.

When I was a first-year student at OBC, the president, Don Earl Boatman, called me into his office and asked me if I would be willing to travel to the central Missouri town of LaMonte and hold a revival for the local Christian Church. I don't think I had more than two sermons at the time; but I prepared several more and went to LaMonte. God blessed, and my appetite for evangelistic work began to grow. Student ministers soon were inviting me to hold evangelistic crusades for the congregations they served with weekend ministries, and God continued to direct me toward a ministry in evangelism.

At the end of my first year of Bible College, I accepted a weekend ministry with the Louisburg, Missouri, Christian

Church. During my four years with that congregation, we hosted at least eight or nine evangelistic crusades; for it was my desire to work with seasoned evangelists from whom I could learn, especially in the area of evangelistic calling. Not only was this a growing time for me, but God blessed our little congregation with a threefold increase in attendance.

Having married during my time at Ozark, it became obvious to Jan and me that when I graduated, it was God's will that we travel in full-time evangelistic work. This we did for nearly six years working with churches large and small all over the USA as well as in several foreign countries. While thousands of people made decisions for Christ in those crusades, most of that was due to the faithful witness of local Christians and the evangelistic efforts of the local ministers. However, it was a learning time for me; and I am indebted to literally hundreds of preachers and Christian leaders who made contributions both to my life personally and my understanding of the work of evangelism.

Our son, Shan, was born during our first year of evangelistic work. The first five years of his life we lived out of a twenty-six foot travel trailer. However, Jan and I were convinced it was God's will for us to go into a local ministry when Shan was of school age. Furthermore, we were convinced that it was God's will for us to go to a new congregation rather than an established one. All of this led us to Kingsway where Shan's sister, Jennifer, was soon to join us. Our ministry here has now spanned over two decades.

We came to Kingsway with the understanding that evangelism would be our primary thrust, and it always has been. Methodology has continued to change over the years, but we are more committed than ever to fulfilling the mission and obeying the mandate of seeking and saving the lost.

It has not been my intention to bore you with all this autobiographical data but to help you understand the context out of which this book is written. Hundreds of people are contributors. Few, if any, ideas in this book are original with me. They are the composite of over thirty years of experience in which far more people than I could ever mention or even remember have shared ideas and happenings which have made their way into this book. Where I am aware of a specific contribution, I've tried to acknowledge the source. However, to those whose ideas have made their way into these pages without acknowledgment, I can only offer my gratitude and my assurance that no slight was intended.

For the past several years, it has been my joy to serve as an adjunct professor of practical theology at Cincinnati Bible Seminary with the encouragement of Dr. Joe Ellis and Dr. Bill Bravard. One of the courses I have taught several times is "Evangelism in the Local Church." Much of the material in this book is based on lectures that have been part of that course. I am also indebted to the many graduate students who have influenced my life as they have participated in those classes.

I must also acknowledge the invaluable assistance of Marge Perry and Mary Conner in the preparation of the manuscript for this book. And finally, I want to express my gratitude to the Kingsway eldership whose kingdom view allows my own personal ministry to extend far beyond the confines of our local congregation. I am thankful beyond my ability to express it that they, too, believe that the primary purpose of the church is evangelism; and they back up that conviction with their personal practice and their support of our statement of purpose, the first point of which is as follows: "The purpose of Kingsway Christian Church is first of all to evangelize the lost, starting with our own immediate ministry area, but with a mission program extending around the world."

John Caldwell
January, 1995

CHAPTER ONE

THE MISSION

On a dangerous seacoast where shipwrecks often occur, there was once a crude little lifesaving station. The building was just a hut, and there was only one boat, but the few devoted members kept a constant watch over the sea, and with no thought for themselves went out day and night tirelessly searching for the lost. Many lives were saved by this wonderful little station, so that it became famous. Some of those who were saved, and various others in the surrounding area, wanted to become associated with the station and give of their time and money and effort for the support of its work. New boats were bought and new crews trained. The little lifesaving station grew.

Some of the members of the lifesaving station were unhappy that the building was so crude and poorly equipped. They felt that a more comfortable place should be provided as the first refuge of those saved from the sea. So they replaced the emergency cots with beds and put better furniture in the enlarged building. Now the lifesaving station became a popular gathering place for its members, and they decorated it beautifully and furnished it exquisitely, because they used it as a sort of club. Fewer members were now interested in going to sea on lifesaving missions, so they hired lifeboat crews to do this work. The lifesaving motif still prevailed in this club's decoration, and there was a liturgical lifesaving lifeboat in the room where the club initiations were held. About this time a large ship was wrecked off the coast, and the hired crews brought in boatloads of cold, wet, and half-drowned people. They were dirty and sick, and some of them had black skin and some had yellow skin. The beautiful new club was in chaos. So the property committee immediately had a shower house built outside the club where victims of shipwreck could be cleaned up before coming inside.

At the next meeting, there was a split in the club membership. Most of the members wanted to stop the club's lifesaving activities as being unpleasant and a hindrance to the normal social life of the club. However, some members insisted upon lifesaving as their primary purpose and pointed out that they were still called a lifesaving station. But they were finally voted down and told that if they wanted to save the lives of all the various kinds of people who were shipwrecked in those waters, they could begin their own lifesaving station down the coast. They did.

As the years went by, the new station experienced the same changes that had occurred in the old. It evolved into a club, and yet another lifesaving station was founded. History continued to repeat itself; and if you visit that seacoast today, you will find a number of exclusive clubs along that shore. Shipwrecks are frequent in those waters, but most of the people drown.[1]

That parable by Theodore Wedel is most sad because it rather accurately reflects the situation in the church of today. When many churches are floundering for a sense of direction and mission, some are asking, "Is there any word from the Lord?" YES! Christ has a message but it is not a new one. It is not a new commission but it is a GREAT COMMISSION, "Go therefore and make disciples of all the nations, baptizing them in the name of the Father and the Son and the Holy Spirit, teaching them to observe all that I commanded you; and lo, I am with you always, even to the end of the age" (Matthew 28:19-20). These are the marching orders of the Eternal King. The Great Commission is still in force. We don't need a new mission, but we definitely need a new sense of mission. What a contrast there was between the limitless vision of Christ and the limited vision of His apostles. He commanded them, "Do not say, 'There are yet four months, and then comes the harvest.' Behold, I say to you, lift up your eyes, and look on the fields that they are white for harvest" (John 4:35).

When the church fails to take the gospel to the unsaved, it betrays the very purpose for which Christ came, disobeys His last command, declines in its spiritual life, forfeits its commission; and in the words of Jesus in the Book of Revelation, risks the removal of its candlestick. To speak of the church and evangelism is like speaking of a river and water, a bank and money, a school and teaching. One may exist without the other, but it is an empty and meaningless thing, a total sham.

This is a book about evangelism and the church. It is difficult for me to understand how anyone could miss God's intended connection between evangelism and the life of the church. But if performance is any indicator, the church has much to learn in this regard. Thus I want to begin with an overview of evangelism as the trust of the church, the task of the church, and the test of the church.

EVANGELISM: THE TRUST OF THE CHURCH

It is an awesome thing to realize that the message by which men are to be saved has been put in our trust. Jude speaks of it as the faith which was once delivered unto the saints (Jude 3). But this faith, all Christian truth, has been deposited with the saints in order that it might be distributed by the saints. Paul speaks in 1 Timothy 1:11 of the "glorious gospel of the blessed God, with which I have been entrusted," and that glorious gospel has been entrusted to us.

That gospel is a declaration. It is not an experiment, a hypothesis, a guess, or a theory. It is a declaration of divine truth. It declares hope for the hopeless, freedom for the captive, and forgiveness for the condemned.

Furthermore, the gospel is a dynamic, it changes lives. One of the most precious possessions on earth to me is a notebook containing the names of those people I've had the privilege of leading to Christ. Oh, I'm sure there are the names of some who only went through the outward form. They said the right words and were baptized in the right way; but they only got wet and the only thing that changed was their clothes. But where the gospel has truly been believed and received, it has made a dynamic difference.

And that reminds us that the gospel is also a demand. Jesus said, "He who has believed and has been baptized shall be saved; but he who has disbelieved shall be condemned" (Mark 16:16). The gospel is not forced upon us; it demands a response from us. In John 10:10 Jesus said, "I came that they might have life, and might have it abundantly." In John 14:6 Jesus said, "I am the way, and the truth, and the life; no one comes to the Father, but through Me." In John 17:3 He said, "And this is eternal life, that they may know Thee, the only true God, and Jesus Christ whom Thou hast sent." New life is found in Jesus; but it is appropriated by faith which is expressed in obedience.

But it is we of the church who have been entrusted with this incredible message. After describing the dynamics of the gospel in 2 Corinthians 5, Paul goes on to say, "Now all these things are from God, who reconciled us to Himself through Christ, and gave us the ministry of reconciliation, namely, that God was in Christ reconciling the world to Himself, not counting their trespasses against them, and He has COMMITTED TO US the word of reconciliation" (vss. 18-19). However, there is little debate on evangelism being the trust of the church.

EVANGELISM: THE TASK OF THE CHURCH

We have not only been given the message but the mission to take that message to the lost world. The one word which most characterized the work of the early church, the one word which is the key to evangelism, is the first word in the Great Commission, "Go!" For until we go we will not make disciples, nor will we baptize or teach them. And while the word for go in the Greek text is a participle, it has the force of an imperative verb which it gets from the command, "make disciples." The Great Commission does not say, "As you go," that is, "if you happen to get around to it." No, it is our primary mission to GO with the specific intent of sharing the gospel with the lost. We must go! Evangelism is our task.

Now there are those who would make a strong case for making social reform the primary mission of the church. It is true that whose who claim a conservative faith, those who have been labeled as fundamentalists and evangelicals, have been sadly lacking in social awareness and involvement. The Lord does not simply overlook the fact that many of us who claim to be His disciples have little or no concern for what He said about feeding the hungry, clothing the naked, and visiting the sick and imprisoned. Surely one in whom dwells the mind of Christ must be concerned about injustice, bigotry, poverty, hunger, sickness, and human need of every sort. But I am more and more convinced that the best cure for these things is found in true conversion, a treatment first of the disease rather than the symptoms. The only lasting social change will be made as we "go" with the gospel and get people genuinely converted.

History will certainly support this. As I did research for a recent sermon series on "True Spiritual Revival," it quickly became obvious that historically, when such revival has occurred it has revolutionized society and dramatically changed social conditions. Consider the fact that prison reforms, the Sunday School movement, the end of slave trade, and a complete moral revolution were all brought about in England through the evangelistic efforts of the Wesleys, Whitefield, and other such men.

You see, true evangelism never ends with the conversion of the lost. The church also bears the responsibility for teaching and equipping disciples. Indeed, the movement, organization, or group that ignores the fuller implications of discipleship is a far cry from the New Testament Church. However, discipleship, for the sake of discipleship, is just as wrong. For we are saved to save others, told to tell, won to win. The early church had it in balance. Acts 16:5 says of the church in Asia Minor, "the churches were being strengthened in the faith, and were increasing in number daily." To quibble over the relative merits of evangelism and edification is as foolish as arguing about the essentials for building a great army. Which is more important, the enlistment of raw recruits or training them to be soldiers? Without evangelism our churches will die by attrition; but without proper nurture they will die from starvation, and there'll be no one left to win others.

So evangelism is the task of the church. But there are two

major methods of carrying out this mission, public evangelism and personal evangelism. In regard to public evangelism, the New Testament writers used the verb *kerusso*, "to proclaim or preach" and the noun *kerugma*, "the thing proclaimed," one hundred and twelve times. In its verb form, it is an active thing calling for decision, pleading for commitment, and precipitating action. C.H. Dodd in his book, *The Apostolic Preaching and Its Development*, writes "It would not be too much to say that wherever preaching is spoken of, it always carries with it the implication of 'good tidings' proclaimed." He also says, "The *kerugma* always closes with an appeal for repentance, the offer of forgiveness and of the Holy Spirit, and the promise of salvation."[2] Paul writes in 1 Corinthians 1:21, "God was well-pleased through the foolishness of the message preached to save those who believe." God saves through the preaching of the gospel. However, as effective as preaching may be, it will never reach the world for Christ.

There must also be personal evangelism. I mean one person, witnessing to, sharing the gospel with, and attempting to bring another person to Jesus Christ. It is not just inviting people to church, although that is a start. But it is inviting people to Christ. The church must become a sending station for soul-winners rather than merely a feeding station for souls growing fat. Every hearer is to become a herald. Evangelism is not complete until the evangelized become the evangelists. There is not the first verse of Scripture which tells the world to come to the church; but there are numerous commands for the church to go to the world.

Personal evangelism, whether it takes the form of lifestyle or initiative evangelism, is the basic New Testament method of reaching the lost. And it can be done by every Christian, anywhere, any time, all the time. Oh, how we need to restore personal evangelism to its place of priority, power, and success in the church. Let us realize that the Great Commission is not only the mission of the church, it is a personal command to every Christian, to go into every nook and cranny of his or her own personal world, seeking by witnessing in the power of the Holy Spirit to the good news of God's saving grace through the shed blood of Christ, to win every lost soul possible to salvation. THIS IS OUR TASK!

EVANGELISM: THE TEST OF THE CHURCH

The early church was tremendously successful in evangelizing its world. However, any honest person would have to admit that the church is not effectively evangelizing the world of today. Instead most congregations find themselves in a maintenance mode where success is defined as continuing to achieve the status quo. *Perhaps the gravest danger in the church today is for its leaders to be satisfied to carry on and maintain services for those who enjoy good preaching and singing and are willing to pay the bills.* That is not the New Testament church. That is not what the Lord intended. That is the church without power that will never make an impact on the world. A church may have a huge membership, beautiful buildings, multi-million dollar budgets, and a pipe organ that is out of this world; but if that church is not in the will of God, it is all for nothing.

The church is the body of Christ. It is here to do what He did when He was here in His other bodily form. He did many wonderful things; but first and foremost He came to seek and to save the lost. The church is in the world to do what He did when He was in the world; and if the church is not true to its mission then it will surely die. And don't think that all dead churches are apostate or heretical. Many are Bible-believing churches that have lost sight of their mission, their purpose for existence. The church that becomes wrapped up in itself and pleasing itself and ceases to reach out its arms of love and concern to lost souls, soon becomes obsolete. A church to thrive must have evangelism. A church will die with the death of its evangelistic mission. Oh, there may be the form, the facade, the outward trappings, but we can't fool God. And He won't be impressed with how many buildings we've built or how many we had in attendance, or how spectacular our programs were. He'll want to know, "Have you done what I put you there to do?"

A number of years ago I heard Dr. LeRoy Lawson relate a story I'll never forget. In 1950 colonial India was debating their new constitution as a new, independent nation. The drafters had written of freedom of religion that "each individual has the right to profess, practice and propagate his faith." There was much debate over the word "propagate." It was felt by the Hindu majority that the Christian minority might use this as an opportunity to make inroads evangelistically. Ironically, it was a Hindu delegate who said the word "propagate" should be included. He explained, "To the Christian it is inherent to propagate his faith. If he is faithful to his faith he must propagate his faith. So if you do not allow him to propagate his faith, you do not allow him to practice his faith." It is sad indeed that a Hindu from India held a better grasp of the mission of the church than many professing Christians in our western world.

What about your life-saving station? Are its members primarily involved in rescuing those who are lost at sea? Or has the time come when the clubhouse, its appearance, and the service and convenience and comfort of its members are of primary importance? Remember, shipwrecks are still frequent and many are perishing. God have mercy on us if we fail to fulfill our mission to go to their rescue.

CHAPTER TWO

THE PRIORITY OF EVANGELISM

The Holy Spirit has revealed many truths to the church, all of them important. However, He has also revealed some priorities. We can believe the truth and still be wrong because of placing that truth at the wrong place in our list of priorities. Even if we believe the truth; if we major on minors and minor on majors, we can do untold damage.

I remember the first time I looked at an Acura. I was driving a Honda Accord (Henry Honda); and at 150,000 miles, it was going strong so I wasn't really shopping for a new car. However, I stopped in just to look at the new Acura. The salesman enticed me to first sit in it and even to take a test drive in a demonstrator. No, I didn't buy one, but I did want one. The things that were options on most cars were standard on this one. It had a soft, beautiful leather interior; an incredible entertainment package; electric sunroof; and a six-way electronic seat adjustment. You name it, it had it.

Now, all of that is nice. But when you buy a car there are some things that ARE necessary; they are not optional. You have to have an engine, carburetor, alternator, radiator, transmission, wheels, gas tank, and gas in the tank — among other things. BUT, if the car doesn't have a STEERING WHEEL, it is worthless. Actually it is worse than worthless — it is dangerous. For a car — or a church, without direction can be a killer.

In the religious world, we hear many areas of truth being discussed. There are movements with Christians of spiritual depth saying things we all need to hear. But it is easy to get so taken up with some area of truth, some righteous cause, or some element of doctrine, that we neglect that which is most important and we forget our purpose, our sense of direction. The sad truth is that the world is going to hell while the premillenialists and the amillenialists argue about who's right; and the charismatics and non-charismatics argue about the use of tongues in the church; and we give our time and energy to the dispute over whether the local preacher is a pastor, evangelist, minister, or just what. I CAN ASSURE YOU that the lost in hell have little concern for such matters and little sympathy for the church's disputes.

I'm not suggesting that we ignore such issues, but I am saying that we should put first things first. And a good clue as to what belongs first is in recognizing what was first with our Lord. He makes that crystal clear in Luke 19:10 where He said, "The Son of Man has come to seek and to save that which was lost." That was His stated reason for coming to this earth. That is the scheme behind the incarnation. That's what His death, burial and, resurrection were all about. Nothing else Jesus did was done as an end in itself. Everything was a means to the end of seeing people saved.

Jesus did not come to raise the dead, although He did raise the dead. He did not come to heal the physically sick, although He did heal them. He did not come to cast out demons, although He did cast them out. He did not come to elevate womanhood, although He did elevate womanhood. He did not come to set up institutions, although wherever He has been, great and worthy institutions have sprung up. But all these things He did were attendant to the main thing He came to do, to seek, and to save the lost.

Likewise, there are many things the church is called to do. We are to edify the saved, glorify God in worship, be a conscience for our community, minister to the needs of the whole man, oppose evil in society, and do many other things which we could add to our list. The fellowship with which I serve works very hard at shepherding, improving the quality of our worship, upgrading our educational program, and ministering to the benevolent needs of our community. We have many members involved in the pro-life movement. We place a great deal of emphasis on the practice of spiritual disciplines. A dynamic small groups ministry is a vital part of our church life. We realize that there's more to the mission of the church than just evangelism. But suppose we really got going on this small group ministry. Suppose that every member of the congregation participated, relationships were being developed, the word of God was being learned, and needs were being met. But small groups became an end in themselves; and in the process, we lost our evangelistic zeal. Would we be guilty of heresy? NO! But we would be guilty of IMPROPRIETY, of wrong priorities — for EVANGELISM IS THE PRIMARY PURPOSE OF THE CHURCH!

Is that true? Are there Biblical reasons for taking that position? Actually there are many Biblical reasons, but I'll mention just three at the outset.

THE MISSION OF JESUS

The priority of evangelism is first seen in the mission of Jesus. Paul wrote in 1 Timothy 1:15, "It is a trustworthy statement, deserving full acceptance, that Christ Jesus came into the world to save sinners." We've already noted Jesus' words, "The Son of Man has come to seek and to save that which was lost" (Luke 19:10). Again in Matthew 18:11 we read, "For the Son of Man has come to save that which was lost."

Jesus could have been a tremendous leader of social reform. In fact, without it being His primary task, He did more to revolutionize society than anyone else before or since. Yet we never find Him advocating overthrow of the Roman oppressors, opposing the corrupt tax system, or crusading for a guaranteed wage for the poor. Instead, He said to carry a Roman soldier's pack two miles when compelled to go one, to pay taxes, and that there would always be poor people. Jesus could have healed all the sick and dedicated Himself to relieving human suffering. But His relief of human suffering was tempered by His awareness that the most hideous human suffering is as a result of the bondage of sin.

The redemption of man was the only business big enough to bring Jesus out of the ivory palaces and into this world of woe; to leave the honors of heaven for the horrors of the

cross; to give up the adoration of heaven for the abomina-
tions of this earth. Any reason less than the salvation of man
would not have sent Jesus to Calvary. Matthew 20:28 tells us,
"The Son of Man did not come to be served, but to serve,
and to give His life a ransom for many." Surely the church
can be satisfied with no lesser mission than that which was
the central factor in the life of Him who purchased the
church with His own blood, and who even now is the Head
of the church.

THE STATED PURPOSE OF THE CHURCH

The priority of evangelism is also seen in the stated
purpose of the church. That purpose is revealed in our
Lord's last words to the church before His ascension back
into heaven, The Great Commission. In Matthew 28:19-20
Jesus said, "Go therefore and make disciples of all the
nations, baptizing them in the name of the Father and the
Son and the Holy Spirit, teaching them to observe all that I
commanded you; and lo, I am with you always, even to the
end of the age." Again, He said in Mark 15:15-16, "Go into all
the world and preach the gospel to all creation. He who has
believed and has been baptized shall be saved; but he who
has disbelieved shall be condemned." And on the Mount of
Olives, just prior to His ascension, Jesus said to His disciples
in Acts 1:8, "You shall be My witnesses both in Jerusalem and
in all Judea and Samaria and even to the remotest part of the
earth."

In obedience to that commission, we observe throughout
the book of Acts that the church was born in evangelism.
Three thousand were saved on Pentecost. People were added
daily to the church. Soon the number of men reached five
thousand. Multitudes more were added. They kept right on
teaching and preaching Jesus publicly and from house to
house. And the Word kept spreading. Soon the number of
disciples multiplied. And then persecution came, and the
disciples were scattered, but they went everywhere preaching
the Word. And the whole process continued.

The early church took our Lord's commission seriously

and set out to fulfill it. But what of the modern church? Are we effectively evangelizing the world? Any honest person must answer, "No!" Radio commentator Paul Harvey charges, "With all our education, our theology, our fine buildings, our image of the church, we are doing less to win people to Christ than our unschooled forefathers did. We are no longer fishers of men; we are keepers of the aquarium. We spend most of our time swiping fish from each other's bowls."[3]

THE LOST CONDITION OF MAN

Jesus, Himself, said, "What is a man profitted, if he gains the whole world, and forfeits his soul? Or what will a man give in exchange for his soul (Matthew 16:26)?" In almost three decades of preaching, I've preached hundreds of funerals. I've seen the deceased placed in the most expensive of caskets and dressed in the finest of clothes. I've seen floral tributes which completely lined the walls of the chapel. I've seen people buried wearing the finest of jewelry money can buy. I've preached to overflow crowds of mourners. Yet none of that erases the greatest of tragedies if a person dies lost. LOST! We don't even want to think about it. Lost! Spiritually dead! Eternally condemned! Separated from God! The object of righteous wrath! Lost! Forever!

It was unlike any funeral I had ever preached. Doug had been killed in an auto accident. With his buddy and him both drunk, the van had left the road and hit a tree. Thrown from the van, Doug was killed instantly. With no church background whatsoever, the family knew someone who knew someone who knew me. When I went to the funeral home to make arrangements, he was already laid out in his Harley Motorcycle muscle shirt. When I returned the next day for the service, fifty big, burly bikers were already parked out front, ready to provide an escort to the cemetery. Inside, you could not see across the room, for strange, musty smoke filled the air. Instead of quiet organ music, hard acid rock blared from the speakers. The chapel was filled to capacity long before the service. Once again approaching the casket, I couldn't believe my eyes. Doug's Harley leaned against the casket. Two banners now decorated the casket: "Ride Hard, Die Hard," and "Born to Ride." In the casket itself, friends had deposited a Jack Daniels flask, several joints of marijuana, and a cigarette lighter. The only inconsistent thing was the white Bible someone had placed beneath folded hands that had probably never touched a Bible in life.

I must admit that those in attendance were the most attentive audience I've ever spoken for. You could have heard a pin drop as I simply preached the gospel of the love of Christ for fallen man. However, that which made the greatest impression on me was yet to come. The viewing took over one hour. Those big, tough looking bikers threw themselves on the body and sobbed and sobbed. The rough exteriors, the long hair, the vulgar slogans printed on their shirts, and all their attempts to appear tough could not hold back their anguish. And I was struck by this powerful picture of what Paul meant when he said to the Christians in Thessalonica that they should not grieve "as do the rest who have NO HOPE." NO HOPE! That's what I was witnessing. Doug was lost! LOST! Don't you see why evangelism MUST be our priority?

And the fact is that instead of reaching all the Doug's of the world, we're actually falling further and further behind. When Christ walked on this earth there may have been as many as 250 million people populating the planet. It wasn't until 1830 there were 1 billion. In 1965, there were 3 billion. And in 1986, we passed 5 billion. Until recently, China was growing by 1 million per month. The world's population is said to be increasing by at least 70 million per year. And the tragic truth is that we are falling further and further behind.

Jesus said, "He who does not believe has been judged already; because he has not believed in the name of the only begotten Son of God. . . . He who believes in the Son has eternal life; but he who does not obey the Son shall not see life, but the wrath of God abides on him" (John 3:18,36). I for one believe that Jesus meant what He said. That's why there is such urgency in the words of Jesus in John 20:21, "As the Father has sent me, I also send you." And that's why James writes in James 5:20, "Let him know that he who turns a sinner from the error of his way will save his soul from death, and will cover a multitude of sins." We of the church have the blessed privilege and obligation of being a part of a rescue squad for the souls of men.

He had had a light heart attack and at 86 was rather weak. We had some really good visits in the hospital. He was a neat guy. His wife had been a Christian most of her adult life; but I had had the the privilege of winning him to Christ when he was 77. He had grown so much as a Christian. He loved the Lord and the church and he loved me and I loved him. Now came the word that he was dead. I wasn't surprised, but neither was I ready. I drove over to see his widow with whom he had shared 62 years of married life. That sweet, frail, newly-widowed, gray-haired lady was unusually strong. I encouraged her to begin to reminisce about their life together. It didn't take much prompting. But then she stopped. "Oh, John, the important thing is that he was saved, he's with the Lord!" And with that she laid back her head and laughed a laugh of delight I shall never forget. Her eyes sparkled through her tears. "And John, it would never have happened if it hadn't been for you. You don't know how many times Russell said, 'I'm so thankful John never gave up on me.'"

That evening I wept a lot of tears — first in my car and then at home. I wept tears of humility that God would choose to use me; tears of joy that Russell's absence from the body meant he was at home with the Lord; tears of appreciation for that sweet little lady; tears of sorrow for a time of separation; but tears of gratitude that Christ allows us as His ambassadors to take part in His purpose in coming to this earth, that of seeking and saving the lost.

Let's get personal. Are you as concerned about the lost as when you first believed? Is the congregation of which you are a part as concerned about seeing people saved as in years gone by? How long has it been since you have personally gone and shared the gospel with someone? Do you truly believe that people without Christ are lost and headed for eternal hell? That last question is the key question. For when we cease to believe that people are lost and thus cease to personally urge them to come to Christ, the glory will depart.

The church or movement that ceases to be evangelistic will soon cease to be evangelical; and that church or movement that ceases to be evangelical will soon cease to be, in anything more than form and name. It is my prayer in writing this book that people might be motivated to go in the power of the Holy Spirit, proclaim the Word, win the lost, and thus fulfill the primary mission of the church.

CHAPTER THREE

THE PROGRAM FOR EVANGELISM

The priority of the church is to be evangelism. In response to the Great Commission of our Lord, we as Christians are to be going into our world, making disciples, baptizing those who commit their lives to Christ, and teaching them all that Jesus taught us. It is interesting to note that Jesus calls His disciples to be FISHERS OF MEN and LABORERS IN THE HARVEST; and that Paul says we are to be AMBASSADORS FOR CHRIST, urging people to be reconciled to God. All of that is evangelism.

Now the way in which evangelism is to be carried out is a wide-ranging subject. For just as there are differing methods of fishing and harvesting, there are differing methods of evangelism, and we see people come to Christ in many different ways.

One guy was converted by someone who came up to him at an airport and said, "Hey, did you know you're going to hell?" "No!" "Well, you are." And the guy began to explain why. That is not the approach I would recommend, but it worked. However, it worked only because the seed had already been planted and watered and cultivated by others.

I was in an area-wide crusade in Virginia in which a local preacher and I approached the house of a crusade attender from the previous night. Before we could knock, the lady opened the door and said very dramatically, "Thank God you're here! Could you tell me what to do to be saved?" I opened God's Word and told her the Good News of salvation in Christ. She eagerly confessed Christ as Lord and Savior; and following her baptism, I joked with the local preacher, "You're really fortunate you had a professional evangelist with you. You could never have handled that one on your own."

Bob Coleman tells how John Vassar was out distributing tracts door to door in the wintertime. At one house a woman refused to take his literature. But this eccentric Christian pulled his coat about him and kneeling on the snow-covered steps began to sing, "But drops of grief can ne'er repay the debt of love I owe. Here Lord I give myself away; 'tis all that I can do." The following Sunday that lady went forward in a neighborhood church to give her life to Christ, saying, "It was those drops of grief that burned themselves into my heart since that old man knelt on my doorstep singing that song." Again, I'm not recommending his methodology, but God used it, and it worked.

What is evangelism all about? How should we do it? What is the right methodology? There is a mentality which sees evangelism as "closing deals." Christians get into contests to see how many deals they can close. I know of one church that gave its staff members commissions based on how many people they brought into the church membership. Another church used to sponsor "soul-winning marathons" where they would gather at the church building on Saturday morning and scatter to the parks, shopping centers, and neighborhoods, and see how many professions of faith they could get. Candy and gum were provided as enticements to get a hearing from small children and to get them to "pray the sinners prayer." Laying aside their failure to disciple and baptize these people, to call such shallow hucksterism evangelism is a grave disservice. Evangelism is not closing deals.

However, God does have a program or plan for evangelism. There are certain elements to any legitimate methodology which we might use. In this chapter I want to point out four of those elements, all illustrated in the ministry of the apostle Paul in Ephesus.

You yourselves know, from the first day that I set foot in Asia, how I was with you the whole time, serving the Lord with all humility and with tears and with trials which came upon me through the plots of the Jews; how I did not shrink from declaring to you anything that was profitable, and teaching you publicly and from house to house, solemnly testifying to both Jews and Greeks of repentance toward God and faith in our Lord Jesus Christ. And now, behold, bound in spirit, I am on my way to Jerusalem, not knowing what will happen to me there, except that the Holy Spirit solemnly testifies to me in every city, saying that bonds and afflictions await me. But I do not consider my life of any account as dear to myself, in order that I may finish my course, and the ministry which I received from the Lord Jesus, to testify solemnly of the gospel of the grace of God (Acts 20:18-24).

PRESENCE

In order to evangelize, Paul first went to Ephesus where he spent time with those he intended to evangelize. "I was with you the whole time" (vs. 24). Never forget that the first word in the Great Commission is "GO," and the reason most of us aren't winning more people to Christ is because we're not going more.

The word, "Go," is not a general suggestion like a cafeteria choice. It is not an indirect implication of the text. It is as pointed as an Apache arrow, piercing the complacency of lethargic hearts. "GO!" Jesus said it clearly and unmistakably. Some think it is enough that they give so others can go. No, it is good to give, but we still must go. Some think it is enough to pray for the lost and for others who do go. No, it is good to pray, but we still must go. Preachers sometimes think it is enough to teach and motivate others to go. That is certainly a primary responsibility of a pastor/teacher, but the preacher is still under God's mandate to go.

Where are we to go? We are to go where the people are. The church is called to be sensitive to people, to be aware of their needs. Christ never called us to isolate ourselves from the world but to be in the world. Certainly it is important for Christians to come together; but our primary work is done not as we gather but as we scatter. All of us would do well to examine our church calendars to see if we have even allowed time for our people to scatter, to go where the people are, and to meet needs.

The non-Christian world isn't interested in religion or the Bible. However, non-Christian people are interested in having their needs met, and they don't care where the help comes from if it is relevant to their needs. Of course, nothing is more relevant than God's Word. But that's why Jesus said we must be salt and light. Salt, to do its work, must come in contact with the meat. It serves no purpose as long as it remains in the salt shaker. Light must touch darkness in order to dispel it. I have often had Christians ask me to pray that they can get out of their non-Christian workplace and into a setting where their co-workers are Christians. But why should I pray for such a thing when in the non-Christian workplace they have the opportunity to be salt and light, and that's what Jesus wants all of us to be. The light always shines brightest in the darkest place.

Why did the early church have such phenomenal success? I mean those early Christians turned their world upside down or was it right side up? But they did it for Christ. And the resultant growth of the church, as recorded in the book of Acts, reads like some sort of fantastic fiction to most of us. How did they do it? They majored on going. You can't read the history of the early church without realizing that the very core, the center, the launching pad of New Testament church activity was GOING into the world to evangelize.

PROCLAMATION

Presence alone will not get the job done. Simply being there and living a good life will not win the world. There must also be proclamation. The ministry of the apostle Paul centered on proclamation of the Word. "I did not shrink from declaring to you anything that was profitable, and teaching you publicly and from house to house" (vs. 20). What Paul taught others to do, he made a priority in his own life.

Paul realized that God only has one plan for saving the world. He wrote in 1 Corinthians 1:21, "God was well pleased through the foolishness of the MESSAGE PREACHED to save those who believe." Jesus put it this way in Mark 16:15-16:

"GO into all the world and PREACH the gospel to all creation. He who has believed and has been baptized shall be saved; but he who has disbelieved shall be condemned." Again Paul writes in Romans 1:16, "I am not ashamed of the gospel, for it is the power of God for salvation to everyone who believes, to the Jew first and also to the Greek."

Not only did the early church GO — but they went everywhere PROCLAIMING the Word. They proclaimed Jesus to individuals or groups, in synagogues, on river banks, on boats, in houses, in castles and palaces, in prisons, and in the marketplace. The church grew as they proclaimed the Word. Again, they didn't major on minors; they were too busy proclaiming the Word. Acts 5:42 is a key verse: "And every day, in the temple and from house to house, they kept right on teaching and preaching Jesus as the Christ." You see, there is a sense in which every child of God is called to be a preacher or proclaimer. The early church understood and practiced that principle. The Christian who did not witness, who did not evangelize was the exception rather than the rule. But today the situation is exactly reversed. Is it any wonder that our evangelistic results and thus our impact on society is so pitifully small in comparison with the early church?

When I speak of proclamation, you may assume that I'm talking about traveling evangelists, revivals, crusades, or at least confrontational, button-holing, "Mister, are you saved?" evangelism. Well, there was a time when many churches used revivals or evangelistic crusades as their only real means of evangelistic proclamation. It was not unusual to see large numbers come to Christ in such meetings because the fruit was ripe and ready to be harvested. It was not unusual even 25 years ago for whole communities to turn out for a revival. But such meetings are no longer the dominant means of evangelism. I believe they are still valid. I've been involved in some very successful ones in recent years. But they are only one arrow in the quiver, not the whole quiver. And while some people are ready to give it a premature burial, door-to-door evangelism is still very effective. We have dozens of people out calling in organized evengelistic calling each week at Kingsway. A *Christianity Today* feature on evangelism revealed that a majority of the fastest growing Southern Baptist churches were baptizing hundreds of converts each year through use of door-to-door visitation. Baptist Pastor Paige Patterson shared this interesting insight, "The average Baptist may not be a personal witness, but he is ashamed of himself if he isn't."[4] I fear that most Christians not only are not ashamed of the fact that they don't witness, but aren't even aware that they are supposed to do so.

The point is that success is not the private domain of a particular method of proclamation; but it is dependent on a determined commitment to proclamation. Sure, lifestyle or relational evangelism is the most natural methodology and has some built-in bonuses. Let's emphasize it. But it is just one means of getting the job done. The fact is, the only GOOD method is the one you'll USE. Someone has said, "There's no bad way to win a person to Christ." Well, one thing is for sure, none of us can plead lack of resources; for more tools and training programs are available than have ever existed before. Let's find something we feel comfortable with and use it.

PERSUASION

Presence and proclamation are basic to evangelism. However, God's plan for effective evangelism also requires persuasion. ". . . solemnly testifying to both Jews and Greeks of repentance toward God and faith in our Lord Jesus Christ" (vs. 21). A whole chapter will be devoted to this subject so I won't deal with it in depth now; however, I want to acknowledge that persuasion is very much a part of God's program for evangelism.

Paul wrote in 2 Corinthians 5:11, "Therefore, knowing the fear of the Lord, we PERSUADE men." And it is amazing just how little persuasion it often takes. Some years ago I was preaching a revival in an eastern state. The preacher and I had stopped by the church building during the day where he needed to spend some time in his office. It was a beautiful day and so I went outside to get some fresh air. A man living next to the church was raking leaves so I went over and struck up a conversation. I learned he had lived next to that church for twenty years. He had visited there often. He had many friends in the church and had known each of the preachers who had come and gone. But he was not a Christian. I asked him if he believed in Jesus, that He is the Son of God. He told me that he did. I asked him if he understood that he was a sinner and needed a Savior. Again he said that he did. I asked him if he wouldn't like to accept Jesus Christ as Lord and Savior that very day and again he answered in the affirmative. I led him in a confession of faith and prayer and then suggested that he could be baptized that very hour. We walked together to the church building and the preacher's study where we told him the good news. The preacher baptized the neighbor. It was only then, after his baptism as he was getting ready to go back home that I asked him this question, "You've lived her all these years, you've attended services again and again, and you've had many Christian friends — why did you wait until today to become a Christian?" Here was his response: "Because NOBODY EVER ASKED ME TO BEFORE!" How many people do you know who just might be waiting for you to ask them to receive Christ?

I've got lots of true experiences like that which I could share but instead I'll share one for which I can't really vouch. It's the story of a young farmer who was drafted into the Confederate Army and sent to fight without any training. In his first battle they were being beaten and retreat was sounded. But he didn't know the bugle calls and so he kept right on fighting. When he didn't return to camp, his friends thought he was dead; but he returned at sundown with a captured Union officer. Astonished, they asked, "Where did you get him?" Well, that was too much for him. He had been left to fight the whole Union Army by himself. "Where? Where do you think? The woods are full of them. Why don't you go get one for yourself? You could if you tried!" His success reminds me of many new converts I've known who haven't yet been taught that they can't evangelize. And so they just go on their way persuading men and women to come to Christ. There's a whole world out there to be won.

PARTICIPATION

As important as the principles of presence, proclamation, and persuasion may be, the most basic principle of all is that of participation. The truth is, every Christian is to be involved in evangelism. Paul was personally involved in the priority of the church: "I do not consider my life of any account as dear to myself, in order that I may finish my course, and the ministry which I received from the Lord Jesus, to testify solemnly of the gospel of the grace of God" (vs. 24). But what I really want you to see is that YOU and I are to participate as well. The great commission is for us. Preachers, I know that someone has said, "We get so terrestrially tired that we don't celestially care." But we've still got to evangelize. Musicians, talent and performance are not enough. You've still got to go and tell. Elders, attending board meetings and hearing financial reports won't win the world. You've got to go. Sunday School teacher, it's one thing to teach about the worth of a soul, but it's another to model genuine concern by personally going and sharing the love of God with someone who is lost.

Yes, we've got to go, even if it's not our GIFT. I believe God does especially gift some people as evangelists and those people are held to a higher standard of performance; but even if evangelism is not your gift, it is still His command. My mother used to tell me, "Son, take out the trash and burn it." (That was when you could still legally do that.) Suppose I had said, "Mother, that's not my gift." The cherry tree switch that was kept behind the door would have come out of hiding and convinced me that it really didn't matter whether or not it was my gift.

One reason I emphasize this so much is simply because, Christian leader, if you and I will not go, our people will not go. You cannot expect others to go where you will not lead. Brethren, we are ambassadors for Christ. We have been given the ministry of reconciliation. If we are going to get the job done we are going to have to take our ambassadorship seriously. And beyond our personal involvement, we who serve as pastor/teachers are going to have to realize that one of the primary responsibilities in ministry is to train, equip, and motivate the members of our congregations in this ministry of reconciliation.

The professional ministry cannot win the world to Christ. It takes grass-roots evangelism. But that won't happen unless those of us who are leaders in the church are first of all modeling it in our lives. The problem in evangelism today is the same one that existed when Jesus walked on earth. "The harvest is plentiful, but the laborers are few; therefore beseech the Lord of the harvest to send out laborers into His harvest" (Luke 10:2).

Let me close this chapter with the story of a pilot, a boy scout, a minister, and a very smart man who were traveling together somewhere over Alaska. The pilot came rushing back into the passenger cabin saying there was something wrong with the plane and it was going to crash. "The problem is we only have three parachutes." Even as he spoke the pilot was putting on one of them. "I'm sorry, I know I should be the one to go down with the plane, but I just can't bear the thought of leaving my family." And with that he jumped out.

The very smart man grabbed the next one and said, "I am perhaps the smartest man in the world. It would be a tragic loss for humanity if I were to die." And with that he too jumped.

The minister said to the boy scout, "Son, you're young and have got everything to live for. I'm older and besides I'm close to the Lord and ready to meet Him, so I want you to have the last parachute."

The boy scout said, "Relax, preacher, there's no need to worry. The smartest man in the world just grabbed my knapsack and jumped out of the plane."

The truth is, our world is filled with a lot of smart people: and all they've got is a knapsack, falling out of an airplane.

Our job as the body of Christ is to reach out to those people and say, "There's a parachute available for you — a way of salvation — His name is Jesus." Let's get on with the job. Let's personally go and witness to a lost world. And never fool yourself into thinking you are doing God's will until you do. Oh, it is so easy to get so busy doing good things, church work, that we neglect the work of the church.

We talk about restoring the New Testament Church. Well, let's never forget that true restoration requires not only restoring New Testament doctrine but New Testament activity as well, activity that is centered in seeing the world won to Christ. People of God who believe the Bible, let's heed the call of the Master. Let's follow the example of Paul. Let's fulfill the purpose of the church. Let's give priority to God's program for evangelizing the world.

CHAPTER FOUR

THE PRACTICE OF EVANGELISM

Surely no sincere disciple of Jesus who has read the first three chapters of this book could deny that every Christian is to be involved in the practice of evangelism. However, the sad truth is that most Christians never make any intentional effort to lead anyone to Christ. Why is that? Why do most Christians never go to anyone with the specific intention of leading that person to Christ?

A 1991 study by James Engel surveying 1500 readers of *Christianity Today* revealed some very interesting reasons why many otherwise committed Christians are either reluctant to share their faith or don't share their faith.[5] These respondents mentioned such things as being too busy, having few non-Christian acquaintances, not being able to deal with tough questions, and our culture's tolerance which leads people to view as impolite any attempt to question someone else's lifestyle or beliefs. Timidity was the second most often voiced reason for not evangelizing. However, far and away the primary reason given for not evangelizing was fear of rejection and/or fear of how people would respond.

THE RESTRAINT OF FEAR

Actually there are many fears that hold us back from sharing our faith. FEAR OF REJECTION is at the top of the list in this day and age when so many people, even Christians, are suffering significant self-esteem problems. However, we need to realize that when we present the gospel we are not the one being rejected. If indeed there is rejection, it is of the Savior and the salvation He purchased for the person with His life's blood. There is no greater tragedy, but it is not you that is being rejected. We also fear RIDICULE, and there is no question but what ridicule will sometimes come our way if we speak out for Christ. Then there is the FEAR OF FAILURE. No one wants to fail. But again the failure is that of the non-Christian who refuses to recognize his or her need for Christ. Furthermore, we need to realize that while we have the responsibility of going, sharing the good news, and being persuasive in urging them to come to Christ, ultimately it is the Holy Spirit who does the work of conversion (see John 16:8-11; 1 Cor. 12:3; 1 John 4:2). What a load was lifted from my shoulders when I finally came to realize that.

Sometimes there is even a FEAR OF BODILY INJURY that holds people back from witnessing. I wish I could say that such a fear is unfounded in our day and age, but that would not be truthful. I've been cussed out, spit on, my Bible knocked from my hands, and I once had a drunk to whom I was witnessing put a hunting knife to my neck and yell, "I ought to slit your blankety blank throat." I was calling one day with a preacher who was knocked to the ground by a fist in the face from the irate husband of a woman that preacher had just baptized. So while we are far removed in America from the "throw the Christians to the lions" scenario, evangelism is not without its physical risks. I've not even mentioned the dog bites and cat scratches experienced occasionally by participants in our organized calling programs.

There are many other fears that restrain Christians: FEAR OF HYPOCRISY ("Who am I to be telling someone what they need to do?"), FEAR OF NOT KNOWING WHAT TO SAY, FEAR OF NOT KNOWING HOW A PERSON WILL RESPOND, FEAR OF THE UNKNOWN, FEAR OF BEING INCAPABLE OF ANSWERING QUESTIONS (never hesitate to say, "I don't know."), and FEAR OF INTRUDING INTO THE PRIVATE AREAS OF PEOPLES' LIVES. I once had a member of our congregation tell me she felt one's faith was such a personal matter that it should not be discussed unless the other person brings it up. Great! That's just what Satan would love for us to think. That way everyone can go to hell in peace. At least it can't be said that we invaded their private space.

For some there is the FEAR OF PAST EXPERIENCES. For

others there is the FEAR THAT YOUR FEARS WILL SHOW, FEAR THAT YOU ARE NOT WORTHY TO SHARE THIS GREAT MESSAGE (none of us are, but God uses us anyway), and FEAR THAT YOU WILL SAY SOMETHING WRONG. Again Satan is an expert at getting us to keep quiet on the premise that we would probably only mess things up anyway.

Sometimes there is even the FEAR THAT THE GOSPEL WILL NOT BE EFFECTIVE IN THIS SITUATION. I've often had Christians, even Christian leaders say to me, "It won't do any good to talk to that person. They're too far gone," or "they're too bad a person." That used to anger me. Now I just smile because I know they've not really seen my God at work. I'm working on this chapter the week following the killing of serial murderer/cannibal Jeffrey Dahmer. Perhaps you know that Dahmer professed conversion to Christ while in prison in Wisconsin. I've heard many people openly express skepticism about his conversion and that of other notorious "bad men" like Manuel Noriega. Only God knows if Dahmer's conversion was genuine. But I can tell you that if Christ can save me, He can save Jeffrey Dahmer. For we are both sinners deserving of hell. Roy Ratcliff, the Church of Christ minister who baptized Dahmer was asked if Dahmer deserved to go to heaven. Ratcliff responded, "No one deserves to go to heaven. It's not a question of deserving it. If you think you get there by deserving it, you don't understand at all. All of us deserve hell. In a very true sense, of course he does not deserve heaven, but then neither do you or I."[6] It matters not who the person is or what they've done; of this you can be sure, that the gospel if received is just as effective for them as for anyone who ever lived.

THE TRUTH ABOUT FEAR

Having acknowledged that fear is the primary factor that holds us back from the practice of evangelism, I also want to acknowledge three truths about fear. First, FEAR IS RATIONAL. Most of the fears we mentioned could be realized. But FAITH IS RATIONAL, too. God is sovereign and is capable of caring for us. Even the bad which He might allow in His permissive will, He can use for our good. Secondly, FEAR IS SIN if it keeps you from doing God's will and God's will includes the practice of evangelism. Paul writes in 2 Timothy 1:7, "For God has not given us a spirit of timidity, but of power and love and discipline." And finally, FEAR IS CONSTANT. It is something you must constantly contend with. I've been a preacher for thirty years and have talked to tens of thousands of people about Jesus, and yet I have to constantly contend with fear of one sort or another. Satan knows it is an effective tool in thwarting the will of God.

FACTORS THAT OVERCOME FEAR

But how, given the fact that fear is rational, do we overcome the fears that hold us back from the practice of evangelism. Let me list for you several factors which are basic to overcoming such fear. First, there is the love of Christ. Second Corinthians 5:14-15 is a great text which tells us, "*The love of Christ controls us*, having concluded this, that one died for all, therefore all died; and He died for all, that they who live should no longer live for themselves, but for Him who died and rose again on our behalf." Certainly Christ's love for us should be sufficient motivation in itself to cause us to overcome any fear. The apostle John writes, "There is no fear in love; but perfect love casts out fear"(1 John 4:17). The very decision to set apart your life for Christ's service should also in itself overcome fear. In 1 Peter 3:15 we are challenged to "Sanctify Christ as Lord in your hearts, always being ready to make a defense to everyone who asks you to give an account for the hope that is in you, yet with gentleness and reverence." A third factor is the joy of obedience to our Lord. Paul uses a military metaphor in 2 Timothy 2:4 when he writes, "No soldier in active service entangles himself in the affairs of everyday life, so that he may PLEASE THE ONE who enlisted him as a soldier." We should delight in doing the will of our Lord, carrying out His Great Commission.

Certainly the ability to distinguish between personal rejection and rejection of our message should help us overcome many fears. Jesus said in John 15:20-21, "If they persecuted

Me, they will also persecute you; if they kept My word, they will keep yours also. But all these things they will do to you for My name's sake, because they do not know the One who sent Me." Furthermore, confidence in the power of the gospel will help to overcome your fears. When you have seen the gospel transform lives again and again, then any fear of its failure is taken away. And of course, the terrible, depraved, ungodly condition of this present world should make us so desperate to make a difference that fears are forgotten.

THE MOST BASIC PRACTICE OF EVANGELISM: YOUR TESTIMONY

One of the fears that holds us back from the practice of evangelism is that we don't know enough and that we will not have the needed answers. Yet the most basic method of evangelism is one in which you are already the best expert in the world — that of sharing your personal testimony. You may never have given much thought to it, but if you are Christian then you do have a testimony; for a testimony is simply YOUR STORY of how you came to Christ and of what He has done in your life.

Not only does every Christian have a testimony but a testimony is tremendously effective. For one thing, people can't disagree with you, for it is YOUR story. When you attempt to teach them from the Scriptures they may argue that "That is just your interpretation." But when you share your testimony, while they may not believe it, or may not believe it is relevant to them, they cannot dispute it. It is YOUR story. A testimony is also effective in that you can subtly say things that might otherwise be offensive. For instance, you can be critical of your own former false belief systems or sinful lifestyle practices, which may be currently true of the person to whom you are witnessing. However, because your criticism is directed to yourself rather than to them they are free to make the application without becoming defensive. A personal testimony is also effective in that it whets the appetite for more. Jesus said that a Christian is to be the salt of the earth (Matthew 5:13).

Although salt serves many functions including that of a preservative and a purifier, it also makes you thirsty. As you share the testimony of what Jesus Christ has done in your life, it should make the person to whom you are witnessing thirsty for what you have found in Jesus, the Living Water.

Although testimonies differ dramatically in their content, all have the same basic three-point outline: what life was like before you came to Christ, how you came to Christ, and how Christ changed your life. In telling what life was like before you accepted Christ, you can use an attention-getting first sentence that communicates well with non-Christians. In a recent seminary class on evangelism, I asked all the students to write out their testimony. One young man began, "I grew up in a non-Christian home. I had no involvement in Christianity and no interest in Christ. In fact, my mother was Jewish and my father was a professional gambler, so I wasn't taken to church much." I'll assure you that he immediately had everyone's attention, and the dry wit he demonstrated also set everyone at ease. In this first point of your testimony, you can also communicate what was important to you, where you found security and happiness (remember, the non-Christian is relying on something external to give him fulfillment), and how those things began to let you down. Personal examples help establish you as a credible witness in the mind of your non-Christian listeners.

The second point of a testimony communicates how you came to Christ. It is especially important on this point that you be very specific. Depending on the specifics, you may want to tell about the first time you heard the gospel or at least the first time it was communicated in a way you could understand. What were your initial reactions? What was different about the person who told you about Jesus? What was the turning point in your attitude, if you had been negative toward Christianity and Christians? What were the barriers that held you back from responding immediately? Most importantly, how did you receive Christ? Be very specific in outlining the plan of salvation. It is at this point that many testimonies are weak. Tell of how you came to the decision to accept Christ as Lord and Savior. Tell of the time and place you made that decision. Make the gospel clear by stating what your decision was. Say something like, "I decided to accept Christ's death on the cross in payment for my sins. I chose to make Him Lord of my life and to allow Him to make a new person of me." Tell the specifics of how you first confessed Christ as Lord and Savior and how you were baptized into Him.

The third point of a testimony communicates how Christ has changed your life. It is important that you not exaggerate or embellish. Simply communicate the specific changes you have seen in your life since receiving Christ. Personal illustrations are very meaningful. Tell how long it took for some of those changes to come about. Explain how you are motivated differently, how your relationship with Christ affects your decisions regarding lifestyle, activities, relationships, and the future.

I want to urge you to take the time to write out your own personal testimony (why not do it right after you finish this chapter?). Write like you speak. Make it personal. Remember, this is YOUR story. Then after writing it out, practice retelling it over and over until it becomes natural. Try to refine it to the point that you can tell your story in three minutes or less. If you are prepared you will be amazed how many times you'll have the opportunity to tell your story.

There are many things you can communicate more effectively in a testimony than in any other way. Religion doesn't save. We are saved by what Christ has *done*, not what we *do*. Life without Christ has no purpose. Christ makes a difference. A Christian has passed from spiritual death to spiritual life. And the Christian has the assurance of his or her salvation.

There are also issues that should be avoided in telling your story. Don't get too complicated. Avoid religious clichés and terminology which have meaning to the Christian but little if any meaning for the uninitiated. Avoid denominational name-calling (always let the truth expose error). Don't get sidetracked on tangents — stick to the point. And if you came from a worldly background, don't glory in your former depravity. I've heard some testimonies which made it sound as if the Christian was longing for "the good old days."

Perhaps you're saying, "A testimony is fine if you came to Christ as an adult and especially if there was a dramatic outward change in your life. But I became a Christian as a young person and no one would be interested in my story." Well, the fact of the matter is that most of the people with whom you will be talking are not bank robbers, murderers, or drug dealers. Actually, it is most likely that you are going to be talking with people who figure they are already Christians. After all, they were born in America, they've never been convicted of a felony, they go to church at Christmas and Easter, they may have been christened as an infant, and they give $100 a year to charity. As far as they are concerned, everything is just fine with God. One of the biggest problems you and I have is in helping people get past that false sense of security. And what you consider to be a pretty boring testimony may be just the thing to do it.

There is certainly nothing dramatic to the world about my conversion. I grew up in a Christian home where I knew who Jesus was from a very early age. But when I was just nine years old I came to realize that I was a sinner. Oh, I hadn't killed anyone or gotten drunk. But I had disobeyed my mother and dad, I had lied, and there were lots of things I should have done that I didn't do. I realized that I needed a Savior. And it finally came to me that that was why Jesus came and died on the cross. He paid for my sins. But He did it as a gift. And while I had always believed in Him, I had never made a personal decision to accept Him as my Savior and Lord. I remember well that Sunday morning at Loyal Christian Church in Springfield, Missouri, when believing that Jesus was the Son of God, I accepted what He had done on the cross and chose to make Him Lord of my life. I went before that little congregation at invitation time that day and confessed my faith in Christ. Because our little church didn't have a baptistry, we drove out to the James River south of town where I was baptized, just as Jesus was and as He commanded me to be. I'll never forget how clean and good I felt. Over the years I've failed Him many times, but He has never failed me.

That's my testimony. It's not very dramatic to the world, but it means the difference between heaven and hell to me. And there are many people who have never thought of themselves as sinners who just might be challenged by the testimony of someone who understood he was a sinner even though he was only nine years of age. With a testimony you can also vary your emphasis depending on the circumstances of the person to whom you are witnessing. For example, with some people I would emphasize my teen years and a time of spiritual rebellion in my life, leading to a time of dramatic rededication as a college sophomore pre-med student.

Maybe your testimony might go more like this. Your friend, Joe, at work, seems to be somewhat open to spiritual things. He knows you are a Christian; and through your friendship, you've tried to influence him. He thinks he's a Christian, but you know he's not. Then over lunch one day, you are impressed that this might be a good time and you say, "Joe, for the first 35 years of my life I thought I was a Christian and I really wasn't. I thought that because I had some spiritual heritage. My parents had me dedicated when I was a baby. I even went through confirmation. I attended church every once in a while and lived a reasonably moral life. But I finally came to realize I wasn't a Christian at all. A few years back I found out what it really means to be a Christian and I became one. And if you'd ever be interested in hearing how that came about I'd sure be happy to explain it to you. For becoming a Christian has been the best decision of my life."

Now, all of that would take less than a minute to say; and for many people reading this book, it would be an honest testimony with only minor modifications. And while it was not complete in that it really didn't get into the plan of salvation, it would certainly be one way to move Joe off of dead center in a non-threatening, non-accusatory way. You're trying to get Joe to thinking, questioning, wondering. You're trying to rattle his cage a little bit. You want to challenge his thinking.

But one of the best and most basic ways to practice evangelism is through the use of the personal testimony. The apostle Paul certainly used it effectively. He retells his story three times in the book of Acts (chapters 9, 22, 26) Personally, I've used my testimony (boring as it might seem to you) hundreds of times. Again I encourage you to write out your story, be concise, practice it, polish it, and look for opportunities to share it.

SATURATION EVANGELISM

Sharing your testimony is just one of a multitude of approaches to the practice of evangelism. I've introduced it early on because it is a basic element of many other methods yet to be discussed. However, when it comes to methodology, I want it made clear that I believe in "saturation evangelism." I was introduced to that term and concept many years ago when I attended a Pastors' Conference in Lynchburg, Virginia, led by Dr. Jerry Falwell. The idea is to use any and every method of introducing people to Christ which is effective. That includes lifestyle evangelism, confrontational evangelism, mass evangelism, direct mail evangelism, literature evangelism, electronic media evangelism, and any other method that can communicate the truth about Jesus. There are raging arguments about the most effective methods of evangelism. However, as was pointed out in chapter three, the only good method is the one you will use. We need to do everything possible to saturate our communities with the gospel message utilizing whatever means are available to us.

This is certainly Biblical. It is reflected in Acts 5:28 where it was said of the church leaders in Jerusalem, "You have filled Jerusalem with your teaching." The method is spoken of in Acts 5:42 where we read, "every day, in the temple and from house to house, they kept right on teaching and preaching Jesus as the Christ." Later Paul affirms this method of saturation when he speaks of "teaching you publicly and from house to house" (Acts 20:20). Actually there are hundreds of specific approaches and many of those approaches are detailed in books like *50 WAYS YOU CAN SHARE YOUR FAITH* by Tony Campolo and Gordon Aeschliman (IVP, '94) and *142 EVANGELISM IDEAS FOR YOUR CHURCH* by Larry Moyer & Cam Abell (Baker, '90).

Dr. Richard Jackson was for many years the Senior Pastor of the North Phoenix Baptist Church. I always enjoyed reading his weekly column in the church newsletter. In one such column he wrote, "Our MAGNIFICENT OBSESSION (emphasis mine) at North Phoenix has been and always will be . . . soul-winning . . . New Testament evangelism . . . the making of disciples . . . the inducting or baptism of those disciples . . . and maturing of the saved. . . . This is not the decision of the pastor, nor is it the determination of some committee . . . it is the unquestioned command of our Lord Jesus Christ." Might that same MAGNIFICENT OBSESSION be yours and mine!

CHAPTER FIVE

THE PROCESS OF EVANGELISM

We have already seen that Biblical evangelism involves PRESENCE, PROCLAMATION, and PERSUASION. That in itself shows that evangelism is a process. Paul is referring to the process of evangelism when he says in I Corinthians 3:6-7, "I planted, Apollos watered, but God was causing the growth. So then neither the one who plants nor the one who waters is anything, but God who causes the growth." Yes, evangelism is a process in which we become partners with God. However, we have thus far looked at evangelism as a process from the point of view of the Christian attempting to win his friend to Christ. We need to also see evangelism as a process in the life of the unsaved.

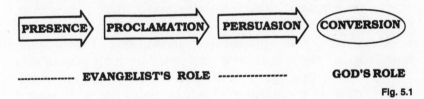

PRESENCE PROCLAMATION PERSUASION CONVERSION

--------------- EVANGELIST'S ROLE ---------------   GOD'S ROLE

Fig. 5.1

Geoffrey Scobie has done exhaustive research on the psychology of conversion and has identified three specific types of conversion; sudden, gradual and unconscious.[7] In sudden conversion the convert made a decision to give his or her life to Christ, most often in an evangelistic crusade, without any prior thought or particular religious interest. However, Scobie's research not only showed such conversions to be relatively rare but in the final analysis to be nonexistent. For while the convert may not have been conscious of any prior thought, there were always some prior influences at work. Gradual conversion over a period of time is the norm in which the convert may move from outright hostility toward Christianity to total acceptance. At the very least there is a conscious movement from not being a Christian to a conscious act of the will in accepting Christ as Lord and Savior. So-called unconscious conversion takes place when a person is brought up under such a strong Christian influence that while they can point to a time and place where they formalized their commitment in confession and baptism, they can't remember a time when they did not believe Jesus was God's Son and the Savior, nor a time when they consciously rejected Him. But in all cases, consciously or unconsciously, evangelism is a process in the life and heart of the person who comes to faith in Christ.

James Engel who now teaches at Eastern College in Pennsylvania has done the church a real service through his development of what he calls "The Spiritual Decision Process" (see figure 5.2).[8] In it he starts with what he arbitrarily calls a –8 with an awareness of a Supreme Being and takes us through the process of man moving toward conversion with repentance and faith in Christ which lead to confession and baptism being a –1. Actually, in the most extreme of cases a person may move from atheism (–10), to agnosticism (–9), to acknowledgement of a Supreme Being, and so on.

The chart is self-explanatory. A person moves from some knowledge of the gospel, to a knowledge of the fundamentals of the gospel, to a grasp of the personal implications of the gospel, to a positive attitude toward the act of becoming a Christian, to a recognition of their problem and intention to act, to a decision to act, to the act of surrender to Christ itself. Sometimes the whole process moves quickly. Sometimes it takes years. Sometimes each step is easily identifiable. Sometimes several steps in the process all seem to happen at the same time. But regardless of the variables, evangelism is a process in the life of the person who comes to Christ.

By the way, the spiritual decision process does not stop just because a person is converted. Just as evangelism is a process in a person coming to Christ, sanctification is a process in which a person becomes more and more like Christ.

Fig. 5.2

Spiritual Decision Process

GOD'S ROLE	COMMUNICATOR'S ROLE		MAN'S RESPONSE
General Revelation		-8	Awareness of Supreme Being
Conviction	Proclamation	-7	Some Knowledge of Gospel
		-6	Knowledge of Fundamentals of Gospel
		-5	Grasp of Personal Implications of Gospel
		-4	Positive Attitude Toward Act of Becoming a Christian
	Call for Decision	-3	Problem Recognition and Intention to Act
		-2	Decision to Act
		-1	Repentance and Faith in Christ / Leading to Confession and Baptism
REGENERATION			**NEW CREATURE**
Sanctification	Follow Up	+1	Post Decision Evaluation
		+2	Incorporation Into Church
	Cultivation	+3	Conceptual and Behavioral Growth
			*Communion With God *Stewardship *Internal Reproduction *External Reproduction
		Eternity	

One of the problems in modern-day evangelism is that most of our methods presuppose at least a −4 on Engle's scale, a positive attitude toward the act of becoming a Christian. That is probably an accurate analysis of most people who choose to visit our church services. However, it is less and less true of our society in general and is even less true in the worldwide scope of things. It is not in the scope of this book to get into the area of apologetics or Christian evidences, nor is it our purpose here to get into the area of comparative religions. However, a recognition that many people are at a −8 and that a significant number are even further from conversion than that requires the church that takes the Great Commission seriously to prepare specialists in apologetics and comparative religions to reach both those who do not believe in God and those whose god bears little resemblance to the God of Scripture revealed to man in Jesus Christ.

NEED ACTIVATION

Now, with a person who is at a −8 or less on Engel's scale, it is Presence, Proclamation, and Persuasion, intertwined with the convicting power of the Holy Spirit that moves a person through the spiritual decision process. But what is it that first makes the non-Christian receptive to the influence of the Christian? What is it that gets the whole process in motion? Most often it is what is called Need Activation. The fact is that people will not change unless and until they want to change. Thus people without perceived needs will simply not be receptive to spiritual things. However, even if there are perceived needs, there will be no interest in the gospel unless it is shown to be relevant to that person's perceived needs.

Thus perceived needs should be viewed as a starting point for communicating the gospel. Psychologist A.H. Maslow introduced the concept of a hierarchy of needs starting with physiological needs, including the basic bodily desires such as hunger and thirst. Next comes safety, our need for security and physical safety. The need for belongingness and love is next. Esteem, a sense of self-worth and self-respect is yet higher up the hierarchical ladder. God's unconditional acceptance of the person who is in Christ can and should be a powerful activator in the spiritual decision process. Self-actualization is at the top of Maslow's hierarchy. Again, self-actualization to the fullest extent is not even possible apart from a relationship with God. In the accompanying chart, Joseph Aldrich shows how God has a solution for man's needs on every level. (See Figure 5.3).[9]

Actually the gospel relates to every area of need; but we must communicate that, if people are to be motivated to move through the process. Perhaps the ultimate motivation is in the simple yet profound teaching of Paul in 2 Corinthians 5:17, "If any man is in Christ, he is a new creature; the old things passed away; behold, new things have come." Remember, people will not listen to the gospel message and respond unless we relate that gospel to their needs as they perceive them.

Jesus was the ultimate modeler of this approach. In the fourth chapter of John He encountered the woman at the well. She wasn't there to have her spiritual needs met but rather to draw water for use in her home. Jesus asked her for a drink, which she provided. He then used that as a bridge to talk to her about living water that would never dry up and disappear. He followed up with a series of questions until she understood that He was talking about eternal life, and then she was ready to respond to Him with joy.

Along with the real needs identified by Maslow and the perceived needs as they are felt by the individual, times of catastrophe or radical change also make a person receptive to the gospel and more prone to movement through the Spiritual Decision Process. T.H. Holmes and R.H. Rahe have identified and placed relative values on changes which impact our outlook on life (see figure 5.4).[10] When the more catastrophic events occur, there is a much higher receptivity level to the gospel as long as it is communicated lovingly and empathetically.

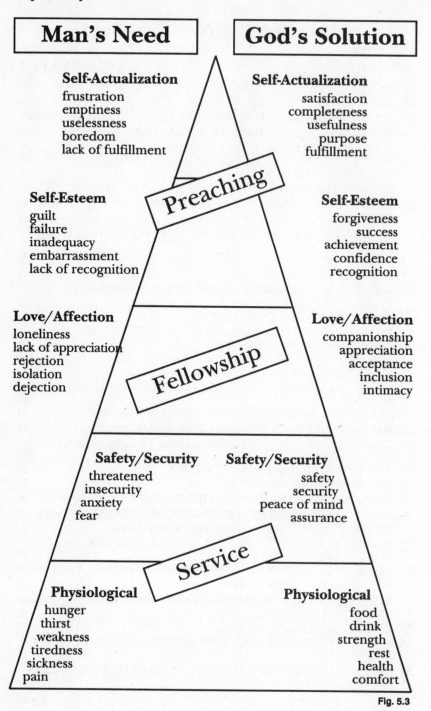

Man's Need	God's Solution

Self-Actualization
frustration
emptiness
uselessness
boredom
lack of fulfillment

Self-Actualization
satisfaction
completeness
usefulness
purpose
fulfillment

Preaching

Self-Esteem
guilt
failure
inadequacy
embarrassment
lack of recognition

Self-Esteem
forgiveness
success
achievement
confidence
recognition

Love/Affection
loneliness
lack of appreciation
rejection
isolation
dejection

Love/Affection
companionship
appreciation
acceptance
inclusion
intimacy

Fellowship

Safety/Security
threatened
insecurity
anxiety
fear

Safety/Security
safety
security
peace of mind
assurance

Service

Physiological
hunger
thirst
weakness
tiredness
sickness
pain

Physiological
food
drink
strength
rest
health
comfort

Fig. 5.3

ACTIVATION OF NEED

LIFE EVENT	MEAN VALUE
1. DEATH OF A SPOUSE	100
2. DIVORCE	73
3. MARITAL SEPARATION FROM MATE	65
4. DETENTION IN JAIL OR OTHER INSTITUTION	63
5. DEATH OF A CLOSE FAMILY MEMBER	63
6. MAJOR PERSONAL INJURY OR ILLNESS	53
7. MARRIAGE	50
8. BEING FIRED AT WORK	47
9. MARITAL RECONCILIATION WITH MATE	45
10. RETIREMENT FROM WORK	45
11. MAJOR CHANGE IN THE HEALTH OR BEHAVIOR OF A FAMILY MEMBER	44
12. PREGNANCY	40
13. SEXUAL DIFFICULTIES	39
14. GAINING A NEW FAMILY MEMBER (CHILD, SPOUSE, OR ELDERLY DEPENDENT)	39
15. MAJOR BUSINESS READJUSTMENT	39
16. MAJOR CHANGE IN FINANCIAL STATE (LOT WORSE OR BETTER OFF THAN USUAL)	38
17. DEATH OF A CLOSE FRIEND	37
18. CHANGING TO A DIFFERENT LINE OF WORK	36
19. MAJOR CHANGE IN THE NUMBER OF ARGUMENTS WITH SPOUSE	35
20. TAKING ON A MORTGAGE GREATER THAN $10,000	31
21. FORECLOSURE ON A MORTGAGE OR LOAN	30
22. MAJOR CHANGE IN RESPONSIBILITIES AT WORK (IN ANY DIRECTION)	29
23. SON OR DAUGHTER LEAVING HOME	29
24. IN-LAW TROUBLES	29
25. OUTSTANDING PERSONAL ACHIEVEMENT	28
26. WIFE BEGINNING OR CEASING WORK OUTSIDE THE HOME	26
27. BEGINNING OR CEASING FORMAL SCHOOLING	26
28. MAJOR CHANGE IN LIVING CONDITIONS (BUILDING, REMODELING, ETC.)	25
29. REVISION OF PERSONAL HABITS (DRESS, MANNERS, ETC.)	24
30. TROUBLES WITH THE BOSS	23
31. MAJOR CHANGE IN WORKING HOURS OR CONDITIONS	20
32. CHANGE IN RESIDENCE	20
33. CHANGING TO NEW SCHOOL	20
34. MAJOR CHANGE IN USUAL TYPE AND/OR AMOUNT OF RECREATION	19
35. MAJOR CHANGE IN CHURCH ACTIVITIES (LOT MORE OR LESS THAN USUAL)	19

Fig. 5.4

MAKING A SPIRITUAL DIAGNOSIS

If we are to effectively help people through the spiritual decision process, we must first determine just where they are in that process. Our responsibility as a Christian witness is to meet people where they are in relation to the gospel. We are then to share with them the claims of Christ in language they can understand, with our ultimate goal being that of helping them move through the spiritual decision process toward commitment to Christ and then on to maturity in Christ.

There are a number of factual factors that we need to consider:

What is their spiritual heritage?
On what do they place value and priority?
Where are they morally?
What are their perceived needs?
How would you classify them?
1) Are they religious but not Christian?
2) Are they Christian but backslidden?
3) Would you consider them morally good non-seekers?
4) Are they irreligious non-seekers?
5) Are they seekers but irreligious?
6) Or are they moral seekers?

An accurate diagnosis is essential to effective evangelism, for the answers to the above-mentioned questions will determine how best to approach the person.

THE ART OF LISTENING

The only way to accurately diagnose where a person is in the spiritual decision process is to not only ask the right questions but to listen effectively as well. There is a real art to listening. It starts with active listening, not only hearing the words, but listening for the tone of voice and watching the body language for non-verbal messages. I've been told that communication is seven percent words, thirty-eight percent tone of voice, and fifty-five percent body language. It is also helpful to clarify by reflecting the person's words back to them, by verbalizing implied thoughts and/or feelings, and requesting further explanation when needed.

Listening is something most of us don't do very well. It's something I don't do very well. However, I am learning. When I traveled in evangelistic work and would go calling with the local preacher, time was at a premium. I would want to make as many calls as possible and thus usually got right down to business, presented the gospel, called for a decision, and moved on to the next prospect. The located ministry has tempered my approach considerably where long-term relationships are not only possible but desirable. However, a few years ago I learned that I had also changed even when it came to an evangelistic crusade, being far more willing to listen than in the past. I had shared the gospel with a young married woman named Lori. I had urged her to give her life to Christ that afternoon. However, her eyes filled with tears and she said, "There's something I've got to do first. I have to visit the graves of my parents." She went on to tell of how her parents had died in a plane crash when she was twelve. She was now twenty-four. Her parents were buried in Western Kansas, hundreds of miles away. She had never visited their graves. For all these years she had carried an anger at God for letting her parents die, resentment toward her parents for leaving her, and guilt toward herself because she was supposed to have been on the same plane. What would ordinarily have been a thirty-minute visit turned into a two-hour listening session as Lori poured out her heart. But by listening we were able to understand her, minister to her, and yes, she did give her life to Christ that day without visiting her parents' graves. But we cared enough to listen; and to feel with her; and to help her sort things out in her life.

Several years ago I came across a very meaningful reading whose author is unknown to me. It's worth reading nonetheless. Take your time while reading it. Let it speak to your heart.

PLEASE HEAR WHAT I'M NOT SAYING

Don't be fooled by me.
Don't be fooled by the face I wear.
For I wear a mask, I wear a thousand masks, masks that *I'm afraid to take off*, and none of them are me.

Pretending is an art that's second nature with me, but don't be fooled; for God's sake don't be fooled.

I give you the impression that I'm secure, that all is sunny and unruffled with me, within as well as without, that confidence is my name and coolness my game, that the water's calm and I'm in command, and that I need no one.

But don't believe me. Please.

My surface may seem smooth, but my surface is my mask, my ever-varying and ever-concealing mask.

Beneath lies no smugness, no complacence.

Beneath dwells the real me, *in confusion, in fear, in aloneness.*

But I hide this.

I don't want anybody to know it.

I panic at the thought of my weakness and fear being exposed.

That's why I frantically create a mask to hide behind, a nonchalant, sophisticated facade, to help me pretend, to shield me from the glance that knows.

But such a glance is precisely my salvation. My only salvation.

And I know it.

That is if *it's followed by acceptance, if it's followed by love.*

It's the only thing that can liberate me from myself, from my own self-built prison walls, from the barriers that I so painstakingly erect.

It's the only thing that will assure me of what I can't assure myself, that I'm really worth something.

But I don't tell you this. I don't dare.

I'm afraid to. I'm afraid you'll think less of me, that you'll laugh, and your laugh would kill me.

I'm afraid that deep-down I'm nothing, that I'm just no good, and that you will see this and reject me.

So I play my game, my desperate pretending game, with a façade of assurance without, and a trembling child within.

And so begins the parade of masks, the glittering but empty parade of masks.

And my life becomes a front. I idly chatter to you in the suave tones of surface talk.

I tell you everything that's really nothing, and nothing of what's everything, of what's crying within me. So when I'm going through my routine, do not be fooled by what I'm saying, what I'd like to be able to say, what for survival

I need to say, but can't say.

I dislike hiding, honestly. I dislike the superficial game I'm playing, the superficial phony game. I'd really like to be genuine and spontaneous, and me, but you've got to help me. *You've got to hold out your hand even when that's the last thing I seem to want or need.* Only you can wipe away from my eyes the blank stare of the breathing dead.

Only you can call me into aliveness. Each time you're kind, and gentle, and encouraging, each time you try to understand because you really care, my heart begins to grow wings, very small, very feeble, but wings.

With your sensitivity and sympathy, and your power of understanding, you can breathe life into me. I want you to know that.

I want you to know how important you are to me, how you can be a creator of the person that is me if you choose to.

Please choose to. You alone can break down the wall behind which I tremble, you alone can remove my mask, you alone can release me from my shadow-world of panic and uncertainty, from my lonely prison. So do not pass me by. Please do not pass me by.

It will not be easy for you. *A long conviction of worthlessness builds strong walls; the nearer you approach me, the harder I may strike back.* It's irrational, but despite what books say about man, I am irrational.

I fight against the very thing I cry out for. And in his lies my hope. My only hope. *Please try to beat down those walls with firm but gentle hands.*

For a child is very sensitive.

Who am I, you may wonder? I am somebody you know very well. For I am every man you meet and every woman you meet.

The process of evangelism includes three parallel tracks. There is God's part — revealing Himself to man, convicting man through the work of His Holy Spirit, and ultimately doing the work of regeneration. There is the evangelist's part — presence, proclamation, and persuasion. Then there is the part of the person being evangelized — receiving the truth, believing the truth, deciding to act upon the truth, and responding in faith and repentance expressed in Christian baptism. We can't take God's place. Nor can we respond for the person we want to see come to Christ. But we can listen. We can make a proper spiritual diagnosis. Based on that diagnosis we can more effectively communicate the gospel in a way which is relevant to their perceived needs. We can use the most effective persuasion possible in helping them move through the spiritual decision process. And praise God, Jesus can save, keep, and satisfy!

CHAPTER SIX
RELATIONAL EVANGELISM

There are many effective approaches to winning people to Christ. It should be a priority with each of us to find the most effective method or methods for us and to get busy using it to evangelize. In his book, *Becoming a Contagious Christian*, Bill Hybels points out that various, well-known New Testament personalities practiced differing styles of evangelism.[11]

Peter was CONFRONTATIONAL in his approach. He was direct and bold. He didn't beat around the bush. Actually that's the style that fits me best. I don't like being subtle. I like to get right to the point. Many people are won to Christ through a confrontational style who would be won in no other way.

Paul used more of an INTELLECTUAL approach. He had no problem confronting people but it was usually with an organized, reasoned, somewhat philosophical approach. I'm thankful for the Josh McDowells and Ravi Zachariases of today who enjoy going into the midst of intellectual unbelief and present the truth about Jesus.

A third approach is illustrated by the blind man Jesus healed in John 9. He used the TESTIMONIAL approach. He wasn't about to get into a theological debate with the Jewish leaders who wanted to argue with him, but he could tell his story. He stated it clearly, "One thing I do know, that, whereas I was blind, now I see." They couldn't argue with that. Nor could they argue with the fact that it was Jesus who had healed him.

The tax collector who became an apostle, Matthew, used the INTERPERSONAL approach. In Luke 5:29 he threw a party and invited all his tax collector friends to come so that they could meet Jesus. He used his friendships and the hospitality of his home as the basis for introducing people to the Savior.

Then there was the woman at the well in Samaria who used the INVITATIONAL approach. When she came to believe in Jesus as the Messiah she hurried back into town with this invitation: "Come, see a man who told me all the things that I have done; this is not the Christ, is it?" (John 4:29). She was a very shrewd woman. She knew that because of her immoral reputation she didn't have much credibility with the people, so instead of telling them she had found the Messiah she simply raised the question and invited them to come and decide for themselves. Verse 39 states the results: "And from that city many of the Samaritans believed in Him because of the word of the woman who testified, 'He told me all the things that I have done.'" Just like those folks there are many people living all around us today who would respond positively to an invitation to a church service, Christian concert, or some other outreach-focused event where they too might come to believe in Jesus.

Finally, there is the approach used by Dorcas, the SERVICE approach. Acts 9:36 tells us that Dorcas "was abounding with deeds of kindness and charity, which she continually did." People could see Christ living in her through her servant spirit and were drawn to Him.

Again, it is obvious that there are many different ways to evangelize. It is not my desire to put you on a guilt trip about your failure to evangelize, but rather to help you find the method that is most effective for you. I once heard about a beautiful new college campus that opened for the first time. An incredible amount of money had been put into landscaping and a system of sidewalks to effectively connect the college buildings. However, when the students arrived, college officials soon noticed that whole portions of the sidewalk system went unused while students cut across the grass of the newly sodded lawn. Rather than try to make the students walk on the sidewalks, the officials simply observed where the students walked. It was easy, for in only a few days there were well-worn paths. Then they built new sidewalks over those paths.

WINNING PEOPLE NATURALLY

Not only is it important that each Christian identify and develop his or her best approach to evangelism, but it also makes sense for us to concentrate on evangelizing those we encounter regularly and naturally on the paths of life we travel. Relational or lifestyle evangelism is not something you go and do, it is something you do as you go.

The essence of relational evangelism is simply evangelizing those in your SPHERE OF INFLUENCE. And your Sphere of Influence is made up of every person whose life your life touches over a period of time, in order that you might influence them for good and the gospel. Actually every contact with believers should contribute to edification and every contact with nonbelievers should contribute to evangelism.

CIRCLES OF CONCERN

Now who is in your Sphere of Influence? Oscar Thompson has developed a wonderful tool in his book, *Concentric Circles of Concern* (see Figure 6.1.)[12] He speaks of ever-enlarging concentric circles much like those caused by throwing a rock into the middle of a pond. The impact is greatest closest to the center and diminishes the farther from the center you go.

The center of our concentric circles is self, for until we are right with God we will have little impact on others. The first circle of influence consists of members of our immediate family. Do you have an unsaved mate, child, sibling, or parent? The next circle consists of relatives or extended family. Your concern should most certainly reach to grandparents, aunts, uncles, and cousins. Next comes the circle of your close friends. You know who they are. Are any of them unsaved?

Further out but still in your Sphere of Influence are your neighbors and business associates. Beyond them are what Thompson classifies as "acquaintances." This circle includes people in your service club, clerks at the store or gas station,

Fig. 6.1

your barber or beautician, and perhaps even your UPS delivery-eryman or mailman. There are probably scores of such people in your Sphere of Influence.

Finally, Thompson refers to "Person X." This is the person God's providence puts you in contact with who you would not have anticipated. Maybe it is the person seated beside you on a plane, or a someone with whom you serve on a jury, or a hitchhiker you pick up along the road. These are the people that come and go in your Sphere of Influence. However, some of my most exciting adventures in witnessing have come with such people. Philip, the evangelist in Acts 8, certainly had such an experience with the Ethiopian eunuch.

Using Thompson's Concentric Circles of Concern, let me urge you to identify the people in your Sphere of Influence. Write them down. The concept will not be dynamic unless it is specific. Why not do it right now before you go any further?

EXPANDING YOUR SPHERE OF INFLUENCE

Once you have compiled your list you may see the need to expand your Sphere of Influence. You can start by praying for open doors in establishing relationships with those who are outside of Christ. Ask the Lord to direct you, for His Holy Spirit to initiate opportunities and break down barriers. Then show an interest in those people. Discover and discuss the things that are of interest to them. There are lots of things to talk about: professions, hobbies, sports, family activities, vacations, current news, current projects, etc. Take the initiative in being of help when it is appropriate. Cultivate common interests — sports, hobbies, eating out. Each common interest opens the door to go deeper. And soon, opportunities to share Christ will come. However, Christians should build relationships or friendships based on giving, not on receiving.

Perhaps the most important part of expanding your Sphere of Influence is in simply being available to people. Availability is foundational to meaningful relationships. And availability includes a willingness to listen. Listening says, "I care," and certainly helps to build meaningful relationships. It also opens doors for communicating the gospel. Ask people to take part in other important events and relationships in your life. Include them in times with your Christian friends, like a picnic or barbecue. Ask them to go with you to church-related events where they can meet other Christian friends. To be quite honest, this whole process is quite costly because you must be willing to surrender any selfishness, truly sharing precious time, places and relationships with others.

If you need to expand your Sphere of Influence and don't know where to begin, let me suggest that there is a gold mine of relationships just waiting to be developed in the visitors to your church. Seek out visitors, welcome them, and offer to assist them in any way possible. Phone the family early in the week reaffirming how pleased you were that they had visited and inviting them back the following week. You could offer to sit with them and introduce them to your friends. You could invite them to your home for dinner the next Sunday or invite them to eat with your family at a nearby restaurant.

QUALITIES OF RELATIONAL EVANGELISM

So there are lots of opportunities for you to expand your Sphere of Influence. Yet there are probably a number of winnable people already in your SOI who you could win through relational evangelism. And relational evangelism has so many positive qualities. For one thing, it's UNIVERSAL, everyone can do it. It's NATURAL, not complicated, and doesn't require a lot of training. It REQUIRES LITTLE BIBLICAL KNOWLEDGE, for in relational evangelism what you are is at least as important as what you know. It's PERSONAL because you're dealing with people with whom you have a relationship. It is SPIRIT-LED, for everything about it takes place as you are directed by the Holy Spirit. It UTILIZES ALL THE GIFTS, not just the gift of evangelism. For in relational evangelism a person with the gift of helps or the gift of hospitality simply directs the use of those gifts toward the unsaved. Relational evangelism also RELIEVES PRESSURE, for this strategy is low pressure and long range. This approach COMMUNICATES THE GOSPEL IN CONTEXT, for your life is what gives meaning to the message. It also OPENS DOORS FOR PROCLAMATION. Remember, presence is only the first step in evangelism. There still must be proclamation and persuasion, but relational evangelism opens doors naturally and gladly. A final positive quality of relational evangelism is that it has BUILT-IN FOLLOW-UP. The new convert already has a relationship and accountability with mature Christians.

ELEMENTS OF RELATIONAL EVANGELISM

We've seen that relational evangelism (also known as lifestyle evangelism, friendship evangelism, and incarnational evangelism) has some very positive qualities to commend it. But what are the specific elements of relational evangelism that move the unsaved person through the spiritual decision process? There are basically three: prayer, example, and witness. All three should be a part of any evangelistic methodology, but they are at the very essence of relational evangelism.

PRAYING FOR THE LOST

I don't understand all the theology of praying for the lost but I do know it is God's will that I do so. I know that God doesn't save someone against their will just because I pray for them. However, I do know by observation that as a general rule those who have been prayed for most fervently have been those who have been most responsive to the gospel. I also know that the Apostle Paul believed in praying for the lost. He wrote in Romans 10:1, "Brethren, my heart's desire and my PRAYER TO GOD for them (Israel) is for their salvation."

As a tool to help me in praying for the lost I have long maintained a "Ten Most-Wanted List" in which I have selected ten persons for whose salvation I have prayed on a daily basis. It has been exciting to remove names from the list as they have come to Christ and to replace them with names of new people the Lord has put on my heart. I have always focused on the top three names on the list in terms of building relationships through which to influence them for Christ. Even as I was putting the finalizing touches on this book, the man who had been Number One on my Ten Most-Wanted List for over twenty years gave his life to Christ. Hallelujah!

But if the Lord is not going to overrule the will of the individual in response to our prayers, then just what is the purpose in our praying for them? What are legitimate prayer requests for the lost? We can pray that God will show them their need for a Savior, that the Holy Spirit would convict them of sin, and that He would convince them of the validity of faith in Christ. Furthermore, we can and should pray that in the lives of those for whom we are concerned, the works of the Evil One would be torn down; works such as false doctrine, unbelief, indifference and hatred, which Satan may have planted in their thinking. We should pray that their very thoughts will be brought into captivity to the obedience of Christ.

Intercession should be persistent — not so much to persuade God, but to stand against the forces of spiritual darkness. It is our duty before God to fight through prayer for the souls of those for whom Christ died. Just as we must proclaim the good news of redemption, we must fight the powers of darkness on their behalf through prayer.

What else can we do to assure the power of our prayers? First, we must be sure of our own salvation. Next, we should rid our lives of any unconfessed sin. When we pray, it should be in faith, believing that God will do the work we are praying for Him to do. Bill Bright has written, "Successful praying is simply asking God to work according to His promised will, and leaving the results to Him."[13] Then we should be sure we are living a consistent Christian life, so that our lifestyle doesn't in itself negate our prayers. Finally, we should be ready to respond when God chooses to use us as an answer to our own prayer. Someone has said, "Prayer is not an argument with God to persuade Him to move things our way, but an exercise by which we are enabled by His Spirit to move ourselves His way." It might even be that the reason you have not yet seen your prayer for someone's salvation answered is because you have not yet personally gone to them and urged them to give their life to Christ.

SETTING THE EXAMPLE

Then, having prayed for the lost, we need to make sure that evangelism is for them a gospel show-and-tell. If we have claimed that the gospel is a need-meeting message that changes lives, then people in our Sphere of Influence had better be able to see it meeting our needs and changing our lives. That's what Peter was talking about in 1 Peter 2:11-12 where he wrote, "Beloved, I urge you as aliens and strangers to abstain from fleshly lusts, which wage war against the soul. Keep your behavior excellent among the Gentiles (non-Christians in your SOI), so that in the thing in which they slander you as evildoers, they may on account of your good deeds, as they observe them, glorify God in the day of visitation." Then the following verses, 1 Peter 2:13-3:17, give specific example after specific example of how we are to live a life which makes an impact on the attitude of our unsaved friends. Peter covers a whole array of issues, from how we relate to the government, to our attitude toward our employer, to how we deal with injustice, to how we get along with our mate. He even gives some very specific instructions to the wives of unsaved husbands in 3:1-4. Basically it can be summarized as DON'T LEAVE, DON'T LECTURE, DO LOVE! Please, go back and study that entire passage for yourself, 1 Peter 2:11-3:17, and let God speak to your heart about the sort of example you should set.

Another passage that speaks directly to the issue of example in relational evangelism is 1 Thessalonians 2:5-12. Here Paul describes his lifestyle when he came to evangelize the people of Thessalonica.

> For we never came with flattering speech, as you know, nor with a pretext for greed — God is witness — nor did we seek glory from men, either from you or from others, even though as apostles of Christ we might have asserted our authority. But we proved to be gentle among you, as a nursing mother tenderly cares for her own children. Having thus a fond affection for you, we were well-pleased to impart to you not only the gospel of God BUT ALSO FOR OUR OWN LIVES, because you had become very dear to us. For you recall, brethren, our labor and hardship, how working night and day so as not to be a burden to any of you, we proclaimed to you the gospel of God. You are witnesses, and so is God, how devoutly and uprightly and blamelessly we behaved toward you believers; just as you know how we were exhorting and encouraging and imploring each one of you as a father would his own children, so that you may walk in a manner worthy of the God who calls you into His own kingdom and glory.

All of this brings to mind Edgar Guest's famous poem:

I'D RATHER SEE A SERMON

I'd rather see a sermon than hear one any day.
I'd rather one would walk with me than merely show the
way.
The eye's a better pupil and more willing than the ear;
Fine counsel is confusing, but example's always clear;
And the best of all the preachers are the men who live their
creeds,
For to see good put in action is what everybody needs.
I can soon learn how to do it if you'll let me see it done.
I can watch your hand in action, but your tongue too fast
may run.
And the lectures you deliver may be very wise and true;
But I'd rather get my lesson by observing what you do.
For I may misunderstand you and the high advice you give
But there's no misunderstanding how you act and how you
live.

I mentioned a man recently coming to Christ for whom I
had prayed for over twenty years. Another man in our
congregation, John Frost, was Rusty's closest friend. John had
also prayed for and witnessed to Rusty many times. But this
time was different. John Frost was dying of cancer. Yet
because of Jesus Christ he faced death without any fear whatsoever. He had perfect peace and if anything he was anxious
to die and be with his Lord. Watching John die spoke more
powerfully to Rusty than the most eloquent sermon ever
preached. However, setting the example and praying for
Rusty was not enough. John gave verbal testimony to his faith
as well, urging Rusty to give his heart to Jesus. At John's
memorial service I felt led to have a public invitation at the
close of the message; and as we sang, Rusty Silvis walked the
aisle and gave his life to Christ. We closed the service with
Rusty's baptism. There was applause, there were shouts, and
there were tears — but these were tears of rejoicing. It was
quite a funeral! But everything that happened went back to
the life that John lived before his SOI. As a matter of fact,
though John never took part in our original calling program,
several people told me at the memorial service that it was he
who had led them to Christ.

WITNESSING TO THE TRUTH

Relational evangelism is also called "incarnational evangelism." Of "the" incarnation John says in John 1:14, "And the Word became flesh, and dwelt among us, and we beheld His glory, glory as of the only begotten from the Father, full of grace and truth." God came and lived among us in the person of Jesus Christ. He was full of grace, and that was demonstrated in His lifestyle. But He also was full of truth and that was demonstrated in what He taught. As important as example of lifestyle is in relational evangelism, there still must come the time, as with John, when we communicate the truth. No one was ever converted solely by observing the life of a Christian. It is knowing the truth that sets men free. But how do you guide the person with whom you have built a relationship, for whom you have prayed, and before whom you have lived a consistent Christian life, toward a conversation about Jesus and spiritual things? First, it is altogether likely that the unsaved person may raise the subject if you have done the things I've just mentioned. However assuming that they don't, what should your approach be?

Let me interject here that herein is a weakness with relational evangelism. Many Christians never get around to sharing the gospel with their friend. Their relationship has never quite developed far enough. Or if it has, they are afraid to say something for fear of hurting the relationship. However, if we are going to err, let it be on the side of witnessing too quickly or too aggressively, as opposed to not sharing at all.

In his book *Witnessing Without Fear*, Bill Bright suggests the acrostic, LETUS, as a guide to leading a conversation toward Jesus.[14] LOVE should be your motivation. ESTABLISH RAPPORT or EARN the right to present the gospel. TALK ABOUT JESUS rather than getting sidetracked. USE STORIES, your story, your testimony, in communicating Christ. Go back and review Chapter 4, if you need to, on how to use your testimony. And finally, use a SEQUENCE OF QUESTIONS. If they have attended a Christian event with you, read a book you've given them, or listened to a tape, Bright suggests the following sequence of questions:

1. What did you think of the concert (church service, book, tape)?

2. Did it make sense to you?

3. Have you made the wonderful discovery of knowing Christ personally?

4. Would you like to?

There are lots of other questions you can use in guiding a conversation toward spiritual things. For instance, the questions developed by James Kennedy in his Evangelism Explosion presentation can be used very effectively in a relational evangelism setting: "Jim, can I ask you a very personal question? If you were to die today, do you know for sure you would go to heaven? If you were to die and stand before God, and He were to ask you, 'Why should I let you into My heaven?' what would you say?" Or you can simply ask the general question, "Jim, where do you see yourself on your spiritual journey?" These are questions guaranteed to open the door to a discussion of spiritual things.

In Chapter 8 we'll deal with actually presenting the gospel. But first I want to take a look at a whole different approach to evangelism.

CHAPTER SEVEN

INITIATIVE EVANGELISM

The case has been made that relational or lifestyle evangelism is effective, simple, relatively easy to practice, and has some built-in advantages over other methods. Unfortunately, those advantages have caused many people to abandon and even disparage the practice of Initiative Evangelism (also called confrontational or prospect evangelism) in which a trained personal evangelist shares Christ in casual encounters, through door-to-door canvassing, or through calling on prospect assignments in a church visitation program. I've even heard people I greatly respect say that you just can't practice that approach to evangelism in this day and age. To say that I disagree with that assessment is an understatement, to put it mildly. Not only can it work but it is working in large numbers of fast-growing churches all across America. Often the suggestion that it doesn't work today is nothing more nor less than a "cop-out" for not doing the hard work it takes to organize and run church calling programs or to challenge people to get out of their comfort zones.

I've already cited the *Christianity Today* study indicating that a large proportion of large, fast-growing Southern Baptist congregations use this approach. However, in 1984 *LEADERSHIP* did a study which was written up by Marshall Shelley, editor, in which the prospects approached through this method were surveyed.[15] In order to get candid reactions, respondents were given the privilege of anonymity. Churches were chosen in Colorado, North Dakota, and California. Diversity of size and demographics in the churches studied were an important consideration. When all the data was in, nearly 80% of the prospects called on felt good about the visit, and over 60% felt the call was helpful or very helpful. Less than one percent indicated they were strongly negative in their reaction to the call. There were 44% who were positive ("I appreciated their coming") and 35% were very positive ("I was very glad they came"). It is also interesting that, of those who accepted Christ as a result of such a call, 80% were in the 20- to 35-year-old age bracket. However, a profession of faith on such a call is an exception, not the rule, for only one of twenty calls resulted directly in a profession. However, calling programs are for the purpose of teaching and cultivation, not just decision.

As a result of this interesting and somewhat surprising study, Marshall Shelley drew out three important lessons. First, calling on people IS NOT OFFENSIVE in itself. Second, we need to make sure the communication is two-way. Too many visitors don't ask questions or show an interest in the prospect's point of view. Third, you shouldn't be discouraged if a night of calling doesn't produce a dramatic conversion. As noted above, the call you make may very well be only one of many steps in the cultivation process, but important just the same.

If every Christian actually practiced relational evangelism it is true that the church would mushroom in size, conversions would multiply. However, we would still only evangelize those in our Sphere of Influence, those we naturally come in contact with on a regular basis. Theoretically, relational or lifestyle evangelism would eventually get to everyone. But the first problem is that not everyone practices relational evangelism; and even if they did, there are some people presently so far removed from any Christian influence that they couldn't afford to wait. There is no church too small or too remote that it can afford not to have organized evangelistic calling programs to reach those outside our Sphere of Influence and to back up those practicing relational evangelism.

ORGANIZED CALLING PROGRAMS

At Kingsway Christian Church, Tuesday nights and Wednesday mornings are reserved for evangelistic calling. At the present time, callers are recruited for a four-month commitment to weekly participation (we all like a specific beginning point and ending point to the commitments we make). Two men, two women, or a husband and wife are given three to four prospect cards in the same general geographical area and are asked to complete as many calls as possible, though quality of call is far more important than quantity. Training the callers will be dealt with in a later chapter. In our program, appointments are only made when the prospect has requested a call. We find that most people will find excuses why you can't come if an appointment is requested, but will receive you graciously if you drop by. Obviously there are some settings where this approach will not work, such as certain parts of the inner city or in apartment complexes with secured entrances. However, in most ministry areas such calling can still be done.

We call on every first-time visitor. The initial visit may be only to drop off a box of homemade chocolate chip cookies and to answer any questions the visitor may have had. However, we make follow-up cultivation and teaching calls, as well as calls where a decision is specifically targeted. We continue to call on prospects until they make a decision for Christ, become actively involved in another church, move away, die, or tell us in no uncertain terms never to darken their door again. I can think of situations where, according to the prospect card, a family had been visited more than twenty-five times before making a decision.

One of my favorite stories comes from many years ago, as you will soon discern. My friend, Dick Laue, was minister of the Englewood Christian Church in Indianapolis, and their calling night was Monday. He had sent callers to a certain home several Mondays in a row and there had been no positive response. Now he was giving out that prospect card again. The callers objected that it was a waste of time and that they didn't want to go. As a compromise Dick said, "If you go tonight and there is no positive response, we'll lay aside the card and won't go back for a while." The callers went to the address, walked up the sidewalk, and before they could even knock on the door it opened. The man who lived there stuck his head out the door and said, "Listen, I know who you are and I know why you're here. For the last several weeks I haven't been able to watch my favorite TV show uninterrupted. But if you'll go away without saying a thing and let me watch 'Gunsmoke' tonight, I promise you that my wife and I will be in church next Sunday." And they were. And a short time later they walked the aisle of Englewood Christian Church, confessed Christ as Lord and Savior and were baptized into Him.

By the way, at Kingsway we have teen calling on Tuesday nights as well. What a joy it has been over the years to see many teens won to Christ by their peers through that program. Today many of those who have participated and those who have been won have gone on to be preachers, missionaries, and other vocational Christian workers.

So initiative evangelism does work, expecially in the context of a church outreach program. The remainder of this chapter will simply detail how to go about making a call in such a program. However, many of the insights shared are equally as effective and/or important in regard to relational evangelism. Furthermore, while much of what I'll mention will seem simple or obvious, it is often our failure to do the simple or respond to the obvious that causes us to fail.

AT HOME

When making an evangelistic call, we should PREPARE TO MAKE THE BEST POSSIBLE IMPRESSION. That includes cleanliness and neatness. It includes special attention to your breath as well as dressing conservatively and neatly, neither underdressed or overdressed for your locality.

AT THE CHURCH BUILDING

Assuming participation in an organized visitation program, it is at the church building that you will receive your calling assignments. It is important that you FAMILIAR-IZE YOURSELF WITH THE INFORMATION on the prospect card, and seek further information as needed. It is always helpful to know as much as possible about the prospect and their situation. Before leaving the building you will also want to make sure you have a New Testament, and any printed material which your church wishes for you to distribute. You'll also need report sheets on which to write up the results of your call, a pen with which to write, and it would be helpful to have some breath mints just to be safe. Before leaving the building a decision should be made as to WHO WILL BE THE LEAD CALLER and who will be the silent partner (more on that later). And last but not least, PRAYER should be offered for each prospect by name and circumstance.

AT THE PROSPECT'S HOME

When you arrive at the assigned home, leave the car quickly and move directly to the house. Don't pray together while sitting in the driveway or draw attention to yourself through loud talk as you are approaching the house. However, BE OBSERVANT AS YOU APPROACH. You can learn a lot about a family, such as that they have small children (toys in the yard), or they like to fish (a fishing boat in the drive), or even that it is probably not a good time to call (extra cars out front).

Let the doorbell announce your presence, but listen to make sure it rings. If you don't hear it, then follow up with a solid knock on the door (don't be timid but don't try to knock it down either). I have found it is better to CARRY A NEW TESTAMENT IN YOUR POCKET OR PURSE rather than carrying a large Bible, which tends to put people on the defensive. Having rung the bell, step back (first making sure there is room to step back) and put a smile on your face.

When someone answers the door, your opening words are important. You might say something like this: "Good evening, we are from the Kingsway Christian Church. Is this where Mr. and Mrs. Harry Jones live?" Again, it is important that you have a pleasant look and smile as you speak. IT IS POLITE AND PROPER TO FIRST IDENTIFY YOURSELVES. They may not be thrilled to see you, but most people are at least glad that you are not a bill collector or someone from a cult. Furthermore, in asking if this is where the Joneses live you are guarding against a very awkward and embarrassing situation that results from being at the wrong house, or finding out well into your call that the Jones family moved away a month ago.

After their initial response you could continue, "My name is John Caldwell and this is my wife, Jan. We were glad to have you visit Kingsway Sunday and wonder if you would have a few minutes for us to come in and visit. Could we do that?" I've often had people tell me they never get inside the house. Yet in the tens of thousands of calls I've made, I've never been denied access to any house where I've asked to come in. How do you get into the house? ASK TO COME IN. There will be times that you shouldn't go in (they have company, they were getting ready to leave, there is serious illness, they are ready to go to bed, they were just sitting down to dinner, etc.), but if you are not interrupting or inconveniencing them you will most likely be invited in. NOW, if you are not invited in, even after asking, don't let their lack of hospitality change your attitude. Remain as friendly and upbeat as possible. Ask for a convenient time to return. And leave some appropriate literature. Don't try to witness in the doorway. If you are invited in, but upon entry observe that it is not a good time to visit, excuse yourself and offer to return at a more opportune time.

CREATING THE BEST POSSIBLE SITUATION

Having been invited into the prospect's home, remember that you are a guest there and should conduct yourself as such. Your attitude during those first few moments will do much to prepare the atmosphere for a good witnessing situation. You should BE AS FRIENDLY AS POSSIBLE. Ideally, your life will radiate joy. Show an interest in the family. Get everyone together and speak to each member of the household, giving special attention to the children. Give yourself to this family. Listen carefully to what they have to say. SHOW AN INTEREST IN THE THINGS THAT INTEREST THEM. Ask questions. I've heard Bob Moorehead talk about "earning the right to present the gospel." If you want them to listen to you, then you must be willing to listen to them. But positively create the atmosphere you want.

As a part of that you can FIND SOMETHING TO COMPLIMENT. The object of your compliment can be anything — the house, the furniture, a picture, or even a child. People respond positively to sincere compliments. By the same token, don't acknowledge an apology. The most immaculate housekeeper will still apologize for the condition of her house, especially if you just dropped in. Any acknowledgment is far more negative than positive. It is important that you and your calling partner GET THE BEST SEATING ARRANGEMENT POSSIBLE for any possible witnessing or teaching. The lead caller should try to be seated as close to the one or ones he will witness to as possible. That means his partner should take the seat that is further removed. It is also altogether proper when you get to a point of serious discussion to suggest a move to the dining room or kitchen table, as long as you are confident that they are clear and that your request won't be an embarrassment to the prospect.

It is also important early on in the call that you ELIMINATE ANY DISTRACTIONS. The most likely distraction of all is the TV. My way of doing this is again the direct approach. If the TV is being a distraction I simply get up, move toward it, and say, "Would you mind if I turned this down?" And the response will almost invariably be, "Just go ahead and turn it off." But let me offer a word of caution: don't do that during the bottom of the ninth inning of the seventh game of the World Series. Indeed, if the prospect is in the middle of their very favorite program, it may even be best to come back at another time.

Another major distraction is often the young children of the prospect. Here is where the "Silent Partner" comes in, as we will see later in the chapter. Every time I mention eliminating distractions I think of a Baptist preacher who told of a call on which he asked the couple to make a decision for Christ. They were reluctant to do so at the time, so he asked if he might pray with them. They agreed, and soon the three of them were on their knees beside the sofa, the preacher being in the middle. He had gotten well into his prayer in which he was talking to the couple about the Lord at least as much as he was talking to the Lord, when he felt something cold, wet and slimy against his face. He opened his eyes and found himself face to face with the family dog who was licking him in the face. Confident that the dog was going to ruin everything, the preacher grabbed his snout and pushed it into the sofa cushions while he continued to pray. Imagine how the preacher felt when he felt the dog's body go limp and collapse. He was certain that he had killed their dog. Thus as he continued to pray for the couple's salvation out loud, he fervently prayed for the dog's physical salvation silently. That's not what I mean by eliminating distractions. Oh, yes, the dog did revive. Whether or not his masters were ever converted, I don't know.

Now, let's get back on track. GET ACQUAINTED THROUGH A BRIEF, GENERAL CONVERSATION. Let me suggest this natural progression. Discuss the prospects' secular life — work, hobbies, special interests. Then you can move to the prospect's religious life by asking, "What kind of a church did you grow up in?" You can next move to the aspect of your own church which might most interest them — nursery, children's program, teen program, singles, music program, adult education — whatever it might be. From here it is natural to move into your personal testimony. This will be helpful in making sure the prospect understands the diagnostic question when you ask, "May I ask you a very personal question? Has there ever been a time in your life when you have made a personal decision to accept Jesus Christ as your Lord and your Savior?" From there you could move right into a presentation of the gospel which we'll look at in Chapter 8. But first, let's back up.

THE SILENT PARTNER

Jesus sent the seventy out two by two (Luke 10:1). I believe that was by specific design. For two Christians working together can provide tremendous support and assistance which makes them both more effective. It has already been pointed out that one person should be designated as the lead caller. Two people cannot teach at the same time. They'll get in each other's way. But that doesn't mean the Silent Partner is insignificant. He or she is the trouble shooter, sizing up situations, watching for possible interruptions or disturbances and minimizing or eliminating them. Basically, the Silent Partner helps to create and maintain the best possible situation for witnessing.

Early on in the visit the Silent Partner can enter into the conversation, helping to create a friendly atmosphere and contributing his or her personality to the call. But as the lead caller moves the conversation toward spiritual things, it is time for the Silent Partner to phase out of the conversation. Their role now becomes one of eliminating distractions and often that translates into BEING A BABY SITTER. On a recent call, the chairman of our elders took three small children to the playroom where he entertained them and they him for an hour while I had a very positive discussion with their mother. Without his help nothing would have been accomplished. Another time my calling partner spent the evening on the floor behind the sofa playing cowboys and Indians with several children while I presented the gospel to the mom and dad. Jim Mast had as much to do with that couple receiving Christ as I did, for without his taking care of the kids the parents would have been thoroughly distracted.

The Silent Partner may sometimes need to REMOVE ANOTHER ADULT FROM THE CONVERSATION. A simple way to do that is to ask that person to get you a drink of water, follow them to the kitchen, and engage them in conversation. I've especially found that to be true when talking to the unsaved husband of a Christian woman. She wants him to come to Christ, yet she wants to protect him from your offending him and in so doing may be a real hindrance to the sharing of the gospel or of that man coming to Christ. I remember one woman who had prayed for years for her husband's salvation. He had finally started attending church and I was trying to present the gospel to him, which included convincing him that he was a sinner in need of a Savior. His wife kept saying, "Oh, he's such a wonderful man, all he really needs to do is just get baptized, he's such a good man." NO! What he needed was to be converted, and no longer trusting in his only goodness but in Christ's righteousness, commit his life to Christ. A tuned-in Silent Partner got the wife in the next room and I was able to lead her husband to Christ.

I've had Silent Partners stir the beans that are cooking on the stove, change the baby, answer the phone, talk to door-to-door salesmen — whatever it takes to keep the gospel presentation free of interruptions. It is also important that the Silent Partner LOOK INTERESTED. Even though you've heard this a thousand times before, remember that your demeanor will impact the prospect. Years ago on a Sunday afternoon call in a Wichita suburb I was talking with a single construction worker. The preacher, who was my Silent Partner, had eaten a heavy meal as had I. It was hot and a little stuffy in the prospect's house. The preacher was sitting in an overstuffed chair, and you've already guessed what happened. Fortunately he was behind the prospect so that only I could see him. But as the preacher got more and more comfortable his eyes began to close and his head began to nod. Soon he was fast asleep. Fortunately he never began to snore. And as the call came to a close, I slapped my New Testament down on the coffee table loud enough to awaken him and the prospect never knew what had happened. But the Silent Partner is to look interested and stay mentally into the conversation, not sleep or even daydream.

The Silent Partner can also PRAY SILENTLY with his or her eyes wide open, asking God to guide the lead caller and give him wisdom. The Silent Partner may also sometimes have to BECOME THE LEAD CALLER, either by witnessing one-on-one to another member of the family, or CATCHING THE BALL AND CARRYING IT when the situation demands. Perhaps the lead caller doesn't know how to respond to a particular question or issue. Or maybe it becomes apparent that the designated Silent Partner simply has more rapport with the prospect. The main point is that the Lead Caller and

Silent Partner are a team. Each one knows his or her part and they work together so that they can achieve the objective of making Christ known to the prospect and leading them to accept Christ as Lord and Savior.

SOME IMPORTANT THINGS TO REMEMBER

In any witnessing opportunity, but especially in initiative evangelism, there are certain principles which should always be remembered. First, EXALT CHRIST. You are there to confront the lost person with Jesus Christ. What they think of you or even whether or not they attend your church is not of primary importance. What is of first importance is that they embrace Jesus. So exalt Him: His divinity, His power, His love, His grace, His sacrifice, His salvation.

Second, TESTIFY TO WHAT CHRIST HAS DONE IN YOUR LIFE. We've already emphasized this. However, it is of tremendous importance that you relate simply, sincerely, and without exaggeration what Christ has done in your life; of what He has done for you personally, for your home, your family, your relationships with others.

From a negative standpoint, DON'T ARGUE, DON'T CRITICIZE YOUR CHURCH OR ANY CHURCH, DON'T GET INVOLVED IN DENOMINATIONAL NAME-CALLING. You have a positive message. Let truth expose error. DON'T RENDER JUDGMENT ON OTHER PEOPLE'S SALVATION. That's the Lord's prerogative, not ours. Besides, it is a no-win situation for you.

If people ask you something for which you don't have the answer TELL THEM YOU DON'T KNOW. False pride is always an enemy. Don't fall prey to it. If you don't know something, admit it, they'll respect your honesty. But offer to find the answer and share it with them.

Another tremendously important principle is that you PRESS FOR A COMMITMENT. We'll deal with this specifically and in depth in the chapter on "Drawing the Net." However, one of the most common reasons for failure in our evangelistic efforts is simply in the fact that we fail to press for a commitment, or often even to ask for a commitment.

Then there are two final important principles. BE FLEXI-BLE. Be ready to adapt to any situation. Become all things to all men in order to save some. And PRAY! Without God's help you will not be successful in evangelism. Keep close to Him. Depend on Him each step of the way.

CHAPTER EIGHT
PRESENTING THE GOSPEL

Proclamation, or presenting the gospel, is at the very heart of what we call evangelism. Without it, "presence" is reduced to nothing more than a good example, and persuasion has no purpose. It is the communication of the good news about Jesus — who He is, what He has done, what He promises, and what He demands — that makes everything else in the process of evangelism meaningful.

Certainly there are many effective methods of presenting the gospel. However, it is important that you have a method, a plan, a strategy for moving the person from where they are to a decision of commitment to Jesus Christ. Without such a plan the person witnessing may spend a great deal of time and effort saying good things but with no result; for an effective presentation begins at the right place and moves toward a pre-determined goal. Where the prospect is spiritually in the first place will determine the sort of presentation you need to make. As we saw in Chapter 5, a person who does not believe in God or who is at a –8 (awareness of a Supreme Being) will most likely need a different approach than a person at a –4 (positive attitude toward the act of becoming a Christian). With the former you will probably need to begin with a study of Christian evidences or apologetics (why we believe what we believe). Having said that, let me be quick to add that if a person will let me, I will make an entire gospel presentation, even if they say they don't believe in God or don't believe that Jesus is the Son of God. There is convicting power in the Word of God itself; and on numerous occasions I've asked to present the gospel to people who denied belief in God, the Bible, or Christ, who after hearing the gospel have accepted Christ as Savior and Lord. Indeed, "the Word of God IS living and active and sharper than any two-edged sword . . ." (Hebrews 4:12).

Now, what method or plan for presenting the gospel is best? As I said earlier, the only good method is the one you use. It is not important that you use what I use. It IS important that you use a plan, and one that effectively communicates the truth. Any such plan will have at least three main points which may be stated in various ways and even in varying order. But such a plan will point out MAN'S PROBLEM, GOD'S SOLUTION, and MAN'S RESPONSE. It is my purpose in this chapter to give you an example of the approach I most often use, an adaptation of what is commonly called "The Roman Road." In this example I will be presenting the gospel to a fictitious prospect named "Jeff." We'll pick up the example at the point where the actual gospel presentation begins.

A GOSPEL PRESENTATION

JOHN: Tell me, Jeff, has there ever been a time in your life that you have made a personal decision to accept Jesus Christ as Lord and Savior?

JEFF: No, not really.

JOHN: Well, Jeff, could I take just a few minutes and share with you from the scriptures what it means to become a Christian, and what the Lord expects from those who do become Christians?

JEFF: Yes, I think I'd be interested in that.

JOHN: I'd like to start in Romans, the third chapter and verse 23, where it explains to us why we all need Jesus Christ in our lives. Romans 3:23 says, "For all have sinned and fall short of the glory of God."

Jeff, if we had never sinned, we wouldn't need a Savior. If we had not sinned, Jesus Christ would not have needed to have come into this world. But we have sinned. The Bible teaches us that sin is disobedience to God. It may be doing those things God tells us not to do (1 John 3:4), or failing to do what God tells us to do (James 4:17). It may even be violating your own conscience (Romans 14:23). But regardless of how we sin, the fact is we are all sinners. As a matter of fact, we read right here in Romans 3:10, "There is none righteous, not even one." In other words, there is not a one of us good enough in and of ourselves to save ourselves, to merit eternal life. Do you understand that, Jeff? Are you aware of the fact that there are many times in your life that you have sinned?

JEFF: Oh, yes, far more times than I want to admit.

JOHN: Sin is disobedience, and, you know, disobedience often brings punishment. That was true at home when I was growing up. It was true in school. And it's certainly true in society. If we break the laws of the land, we must pay the consequences. Now, Jeff, the same thing is true in our relationship with God. In Romans 6, verse 23, it says, "For the wages of sin is death." Wages are what we earn, and the Bible tells us that what we've earned by our sin is death. Now when you and I hear the word "death" we automatically think of physical death; but the fact of the matter is that we are all going to die physically someday anyway. Jeff, when the Bible uses the word "death" it always means separation, as in physical death when the spirit is separated from the body. But it also means spiritual death, which is separation of man from God. In other words, you and I were born into this world sinless and innocent. We hadn't sinned. We didn't know what sin was. But there came a time in our life in which we chose to disobey God, and when we disobeyed Him, we separated ourselves from God. We were no longer sinless and innocent.

Perhaps you remember the story of Adam and Eve in the Garden of Eden. God created man perfect, and man had perfect fellowship with God. But God told man that if he ate of the fruit of the tree of knowledge of good and evil that he would surely die. When Adam and Eve ate of the forbidden fruit, Jeff, they didn't fall over dead physically that day, but they did die spiritually. Whereas, before they had had a perfect relationship with God, now they tried to hide from God. So it is in your life and mine. When we sin, sin comes between us and a holy God. We cannot have that fellowship that God intended for us to have with Him, and so, if man dies spiritually and he continues spiritually dead, and he dies physically, he will also die eternally. Jeff, that's what hell is, eternal separation from God. There are many horrible things in the Bible about hell, but the worst is to be separated from God, His mercy, His grace, His love, His presence, for all eternity.

So it looks pretty bad if you stop right there in Romans 6:23 with what we've already read, "The wages of sin is death," because we've already admitted that we have sinned. But the verse doesn't end there. It goes on and says, "BUT the free gift of God is eternal life in Christ Jesus our Lord." In other words, God offers us not what we deserve, not what we've earned, but what He in His love and grace wants to provide for us, the forgiveness of our sins and eternal life in heaven with Him.

Now it seems there is a conflict here. On the one hand we have the justice of God that says that sin must be punished. On the other hand we have the love and the grace of God that says that God wants to forgive man of his sins and give him eternal life. How can this conflict be resolved?

Well, God solved that conflict, and His solution to it is described in Romans 5:8 where we read, "But God demonstrates His own love towards us, in that while we were yet sinners, Christ died for us."

Now, Jeff, we've already admitted that you and I have sinned. Isn't that right?

JEFF: Yes, that's right.

JOHN: And the Bible tells us that the wages of our sin is — what?

JEFF: The wages of our sin is death.

JOHN: That's right. And now, the Bible tells us Christ did what for us?

JEFF: He died for us.

JOHN: That's right, Jeff. You and I have sinned. You and I deserve the penalty for our sin; but Jesus Christ, the perfect Son of God, took the penalty upon Himself when He died as our substitute upon the cross. That's really what Christianity is all about . . . the righteous, perfect Son of God, dying for sinful man, that we might be saved. My, God had to love us a whole lot to do that for us, didn't He, Jeff?

JEFF: Yes, He did.

JOHN: Jeff, sometimes I use this illustration to explain what God did for us. Let's suppose I'm out here on the highway and I'm driving along not paying much attention to what I'm doing. All of a sudden I hear a siren, and glancing into my rearview mirror I see that there's a state policeman right behind me. I pull to the side of the road and the policeman comes up to me and says, "You're in a pretty big hurry, aren't you fella!" I explain that I really wasn't paying attention and I don't even know how fast I was going. So he proceeds to tell me that I was doing seventy miles per hour in a fifty-five zone, and he goes on to write me out a speeding ticket. While he's writing I ask, "Officer, how much is this going to cost me?" And I really don't know what it would be but let's suppose that he says that the court costs and fine will probably be $120. While I'm sitting there trying to figure out where I'm going to come up with an extra $120, Fred (name some mutual acquaintance) comes driving up behind me, gets out of his car, and comes up to me and says, "John, what's the matter?" And I say, "Fred, I got stopped for speeding." He says, "Were you speeding?" And I reply, "Yes, I'm afraid that I was." "Well, I see the officer is writing you out a ticket. What's it going to cost you?" asks Fred. And I respond that it's going to cost me $120. And Fred says, "Man, I hate for you to have to pay a $120 fine." And I say, "Yeah, I hate to pay it, too, but I broke the law and I have to pay the fine." But Fred says, "No, I'll tell you what I'm going to do." And with that he reaches in his pocket and takes out his billfold and counts out six twenty-dollar bills, and says, "Here, I want to pay the fine for you."

Now Jeff, that's sort of a silly little story, because you and I both know that Fred wouldn't have $120 in his billfold in the first place. But supposing that story were true, let me ask you a few questions about it. Who broke the law, Jeff?

JEFF: Well, you did.

JOHN: That's right, Jeff, and who deserved to pay the fine?

JEFF: You did.

JOHN: Right again. But who paid the fine?

JEFF: Fred paid the fine.

JOHN: That's right. Did Fred deserve to pay the fine?

JEFF: No, he wasn't the one breaking the law.

JOHN: That's right. He didn't deserve to pay the fine, at least not this time, but he paid it anyway. Now, here's the main question: was the law satisfied?

JEFF: Well, yes, I suppose it was because the penalty was paid.

JOHN: That's exactly right, Jeff. The penalty was paid. And it's the same way with what Jesus Christ has done for us. You and I are the ones who have sinned. And you and I are the ones who deserve the penalty for our sins, death. But Jesus Christ, as the sinless Son of God, took our place and paid the penalty for us.

Now, one other thing we need to realize is that Jesus did this for us as a gift. Here in Romans 6:23 it says, "The wages of sin IS death, but the FREE GIFT of God is eternal life in Christ Jesus our Lord." Jeff, with any gift, if someone wants to give you a gift, what do you have to do before the gift will do you any good?

JEFF: Well, I guess you would have to accept it, you would have to take it.

JOHN: That's exactly right, Jeff. And the same thing is true with what Jesus Christ has done for us. Jesus died for every man, woman, and child that ever lived, but that doesn't mean that everyone will be saved. For the simple fact of the matter is that not everyone is willing to accept the gift.

Let me go back to that silly little story I told a moment ago. Even if Fred did offer to pay the fine for me, I wouldn't have to accept his gift, would I?

JEFF: No, I guess not.

JOHN: As a matter of fact, I might say, "Fred, I appreciate the offer, but I'll pay my own fine. I don't want to feel obligated to you. I don't want to feel like I'm indebted to you. I'll just pay my own fine." I could do that, couldn't I, Jeff?

JEFF: Well, sure you could.

JOHN: However, Jeff, if I refuse to accept the payment that Fred offered, then who would be responsible for paying the fine?

JEFF: Well, you would, of course.

JOHN: That's right. And so, when it comes to this matter of accepting what Christ has offered for us, we need to realize that if we don't accept His offer, then we stand responsible for the payment for our sin. So surely anyone can see the wisdom of accepting what Christ offers by His grace.

So let's turn to Romans, the tenth chapter, where in verses nine and ten the Apostle Paul explains to us how we can accept this gift that Christ offers to us. Let's just read these two verses and then let's talk about what they say to us.

Paul writes, "If you confess with your mouth Jesus as Lord, and believe in your heart that God raised Him from the dead, you shall be saved; for with the heart man believes, resulting in righteousness, and with the mouth he confesses, resulting in salvation."

Now, Jeff, he says that you are to confess with your mouth Jesus as Lord. But what does that mean? Does that just mean saying, "Jesus is Lord!"? Does it mean just walking down a church aisle and saying the words, "I believe that Jesus is the Christ, the Son of the Living God"?

No, that's not what it means at all, Jeff. Jesus said, "Not everyone who says to Me, 'Lord, Lord,' will enter the kingdom of heaven; but he who does the will of My Father who is in heaven" (Matthew 7:21). Another time Jesus said, "Why do you call Me, 'Lord, Lord,' and do not do what I say?" (Luke 6:46). So Paul obviously doesn't mean just saying the words.

JEFF: Then what does it mean?

JOHN: First we need to understand what the word, "lord" means, Jeff. The word "lord" means, owner, controller, or master. We use the word today in regard to a landlord. A landlord is someone who owns property and as the owner of that property he may do with it whatever he wishes. He can sell it. He can rent or lease it. He can build on it. He can do with it whatever he wants because it is his property. And so it is, Jeff, that when you confess Jesus Christ as Lord, you are acknowledging His Lordship in your life. You are saying, "Jesus Christ, take control of my life." Do you understand that, Jeff? Does that make sense to you?

JEFF: Yes, I believe it does.

JOHN: Then it says, Jeff, that we must believe in our heart that God raised Jesus from the dead. Elsewhere in the Bible it tells us that we must believe that Jesus is the Son of God. Here we are told to believe that God raised Him from the dead. But the fact is that the resurrection of Jesus Christ is the greatest proof there is for the fact that He is the Son of God.

There are many proofs that Jesus is the Son of God. There is fulfilled prophecy. There's the perfect life that Jesus lived. There are the miracles that Jesus performed. There are the transformed lives of His disciples. But the greatest proof of all that Jesus Christ is who He claimed to be is the fact that Jesus arose from the dead on the third day, just like He said He would do.

And so, we are to confess with our mouth Jesus as Lord — acknowledge His Lordship; and we are to believe in our heart that God raised Him from the dead — that is, believe that Jesus is who He claimed to be, the very Son of God, as proven by His resurrection.

But then Paul qualifies this belief that leads to salvation. He says in verse ten, "For with the heart man believes, resulting in righteousness." In other words, this faith that leads to salvation is more than just an intellectual faith. It is more than simply believing that there was a man named Jesus who lived almost two thousand years ago, or even believing that He died on a cross for our sins, was buried, and rose again. It is a belief which is a life-changing belief, a life-changing faith, a belief which results in righteousness.

Let me illustrate it this way for you. This chair over here in your living room looks to me like it would hold me up if I sat in it. Now, I've never sat in it, but I honestly believe that it would hold me up. It looks like a good sturdy chair. It is here in your living room where it looks like you expect people to sit in it. I believe that chair would hold me up; but my belief in that chair does me absolutely no good unless I do what?

JEFF: Unless you sit in it.

JOHN: That's right. Until I sit in it, my belief in that chair, no matter how sincere, does me no good whatsoever. And the same thing is true with Jesus Christ. I can believe all the right things about Jesus; but until I put my trust in Him, until I commit my life to Him, my belief in Him does me no good.

Let me tell you another story which illustrates this same principle. It's a true story. It happened back in the 1800's up at Niagara Falls where a great tightrope walker and acrobat named Blondin was putting on a magnificent display of daring. He stretched a rope across the Niagara River down below the Falls, across the gorge, where it was hundreds of feet from the tightrope down to the swirling waters and the rocks below. He would walk across that rope and do marvelous stunts. Finally the day came in which he said he was going to do something that had never been done before, and a huge crowd gathered to watch. First of all, he did some of the stunts he had done before. He walked across the rope with a balance pole. He would stop and do handstands and all those other incredible things such performers do. But finally he put on the show everyone had been waiting for. Blondin took a wheelbarrow, (I've seen it. It's in a museum next to the gorge on the Canadian side of the river.) and he pushed the wheelbarrow across the rope high above the Niagara River and the whirlpools and the rocks. He pushed the wheelbarrow across and then turned around and pushed it back to the crowd that went wild with applause. He asked the crowd if they thought he could do it again and, of course, they all said they were certain he could do it. He asked them again and again, "Do you really believe I can do it?" "Yes, Blondin, we believe," they said, "We believe you can do it again!" Finally, after he had made his point, Blondin spoke to the crowd and said, "If you really believe I can do it again, which one of you will be the first to get into the wheelbarrow?"

You see, Jeff, there's quite a difference between saying you believe when that belief makes no impact on your life, and believing with a commitment that means the difference between life and death; or in this case, eternal life and eternal death. The belief that leads to salvation is a commitment of your life to the Lord, a life-changing belief in which you turn your back on sin and decide to live for the Savior.

Now, Jeff, when you've come to that point in your life that you truly do believe that Jesus is the Son of God, and you do want to make Him Lord of your life, and you're willing to trust Him completely, He has given you a beautiful way to demonstrate that faith and commitment. Back here in Romans the sixth chapter, the Apostle Paul is writing to people who are already Christians. They had accepted Jesus as their Savior. They had already been baptized into Christ. But Paul is explaining to them what had already happened in their life. Beginning with verse one of Romans 6, Paul writes, "What shall we say then? Are we to continue in sin that grace might increase? May it never be! How shall we who died to sin still live in it?"

Okay, Jeff, he's talking here about this decision that we've just been talking about, of making Jesus Lord of your life. When you decide to give Jesus control of your life, that means that your old life, the life that you ran, the life that you did your own way, is dead and gone; it's left behind.

Now, notice what he says in verse three, "Or do you not know that all of us who have been baptized into Christ Jesus have been baptized into His death." All right, Jeff, let's stop right here and review. You and I have sinned, right?

JEFF: That's right.

JOHN: And the Bible says that the wages of sin is what?

JEFF: The wages of sin is death.

JOHN: That's right. And what is it that Jesus Christ did for us?

JEFF: He died for us on the cross.

JOHN: Right again! Now, Jeff, notice that when you and I, believing that Jesus is the Son of God, give our lives to Him, make Him Lord of our life and are baptized, we are baptized into His — what?

JEFF: Into His death.

JOHN: That's right. You see, this is the significance of baptism. Baptism is an expression of our faith in the work of Jesus Christ upon the cross by which He purchased our salvation. Obviously, there's no salvation in the water. There's not enough water in the Atlantic and Pacific Oceans combined to take away even one sin. But when I believe in Jesus, decide to make Him Lord of my life, commit my life to Him, and am baptized into Him, my baptism is into His death.

Paul goes on to say, "Therefore, we have been buried with Him through baptism into death, in order that as Christ was raised from the dead through the glory of the Father, so we too might walk in newness of life."

Jeff, this is a newness of life, not because a person has decided to live a good life or because they've decided to stop doing the bad things and start doing the good things, or because they got baptized or joined the church. This is a new life because through the blood of Christ shed on the cross, all of your past sins are forgiven and God's Spirit comes to live in your life to help you be a Christian, to help you live for Jesus, to do what He wants you to do, and to be what He wants you to be.

Jeff, does all of that make sense to you?

JEFF: Well, yes, it really does.

JOHN: That's great, Jeff. But you know, Jeff, someone has said that a picture is worth a thousand words. So let me show you a word picture of someone becoming a Christian. Here in the Book of Romans we've looked at all the principles that are involved in becoming a Christian. But the Book of Acts is a history book; and it tells us about people becoming Christians — sometimes just one, sometimes thousands, sometimes a family. But the story I want to share with you concerns just one man and is found in Acts Chapter 8.

Now the story begins with verse 26, but let me just tell you part of the story rather than taking the time to read all of it. The story concerns a man from Ethiopia. He was the treasurer of the queen and he had been up to Jerusalem and now was on his way home, back to Ethiopia, riding in a chariot. He was not a Christian, but he was searching for the truth and his search for the truth had led him to the Bible. They didn't have the New Testament in those days, but they had the Old Testament; and in particular he was reading from the Old Testament prophet Isaiah. He was reading from Isaiah the fifty-third chapter where Isaiah, who lived over seven hundred years before Jesus was born, prophesied about how Jesus would die for our sins on the cross. God led a Christian man named Philip to come up to him as the Ethiopian man was riding along, and Philip said to him, "I see that you're reading the Bible. Do you understand it?" And the man said, "No, I need some help. Can you help me?" Philip said, "I'll be glad to." And so he got into the chariot with the man from Ethiopia and they continued to ride along, reading from the Scriptures.

Now, keep in mind that this man had never heard of Jesus Christ before. He didn't realize that the prophecy had been fulfilled. But as they are riding along, it says here in Acts 8:35 that "Philip opened his mouth, and beginning from this scripture he preached Jesus to him." Right there out of the book of Isaiah he preached Jesus to him.

Jeff, I don't know what all he told him about Jesus. I would imagine he told him the same basic things that we've been talking about here today: that Jesus is the Son of God, that He died for our sins on the cross, that He was buried and arose again the third day, that He wants to be our Savior, and that He can and will save anyone who accepts Him as such. But whatever he said to him, and however long he talked to him, Philip obviously convinced this man of his need for Jesus. Because verse thirty-six says, "And as they went along the road they came to some water; and the eunuch said, 'Look! Water! What prevents me from being baptized?'" Jeff, I want you to notice that the Bible does not say Philip preached baptism to him. It says he preached Jesus to him. But when we talk about Jesus, when we preach Jesus, we have to talk about the things that Jesus would have us to do. One of those things is to be baptized as an expression of our faith. So this Ethiopian man is saying, "I want to become a Christian. I want to accept this Jesus as my Savior. I want to do what He would have me to do."

And so, notice what Philip said to him in verse thirty-seven: "Philip said, 'If you believe with all your heart, you may.'" In other words, just getting baptized isn't going to do you any good, unless you first truly believe in Jesus and have decided to make Him Lord of your life. So the Ethiopian answered, "I believe that Jesus Christ is the Son of God."

So verse thirty-eight says, "He ordered the chariot to stop and they both went down into the water, Philip as well as the eunuch (the Ethiopian) and he baptized him. And when they came up out of the water, the Spirit of the Lord snatched Philip away, and the eunuch saw him no more, but he went on his way rejoicing."

Wow! He had something to rejoice about, didn't he. His sins were forgiven. He had a right relationship with God, and he was able to go on his way rejoicing.

Jeff, let's put you into that story. This man wasn't a Christian, but he was searching for the truth. Jeff, you've told me today that you've never accepted Jesus as your Lord and Savior. In other words, you don't claim to be a Christian either. But I know that you are searching for the truth, aren't you?

JEFF: Yes, I am.

JOHN: Your search for the truth has led you to the church where you have been attending. It's led you to the Bible, just like this man's search for the truth led him to the Bible. Now Jeff, this man didn't fully understand the Bible, and so God arranged for a Christian man to help him understand. I think, in very much the same way, it is God's will for me to be here with you today, talking to you from the Bible. Now, as Philip talked to him about Jesus, this man was hearing about Jesus for the very first time. Jeff, you're way ahead of this man from Ethiopia in that regard, because you've heard about Jesus all of your life, haven't you?

JEFF: Yes, I have.

JOHN: As a matter of fact, no one could grow up in America without hearing about Jesus. But this man, although it was the first time he had ever heard about Jesus, he came to believe in Him, that He was the Son of God. Now Jeff, let me ask you this question. Don't you really believe in Jesus, that He is the Son of God?

JEFF: Yes, I do.

JOHN: Jeff, when this man came to believe in Jesus, his belief led him to want to accept Jesus as his Lord and Savior, to live for Jesus, to be what Jesus would have him to be, and to do what Jesus would have him to do. Jeff, don't you really want to be a Christian and live for Christ?

JEFF: Yes, I really do.

JOHN: Well, Jeff, when the man in the story we read came to believe in Jesus, and came to the point in his life that he wanted to accept Jesus as his Lord and Savior, what did he do next?

JEFF: Well, I guess he confessed his faith in Jesus and was baptized.

JOHN: That's exactly right, Jeff. He confessed his faith in Jesus. He said, "I believe that Jesus Christ is the Son of God." And on that basis he was baptized into Jesus.

Jeff, you've told me that you do believe Jesus is the Son of God. You've told me that you really do desire to accept Him as your Lord and your Savior. Jeff, you could make that decision right here and now. Wouldn't you like to do that this very moment?

JEFF: Yes, I would.

JOHN: Jeff, take my hand, and let me word a confession for you, but if you really believe it, then repeat it after me. I believe that Jesus is the Christ —

JEFF: I believe that Jesus is the Christ —

JOHN: — the Son of the Living God —

JEFF: — the Son of the Living God —

JOHN: — and I now accept Him —

JEFF: — and I now accept Him —

JOHN: — as my Lord and my personal Savior.

JEFF: — as my Lord and my personal Savior.

JOHN: Amen! You really mean that, don't you, Jeff?

JEFF: I sure do!

JOHN: Jeff, let's pray together. Heavenly Father, I thank

you so much that Jeff has come to believe in Jesus as your Son. He's come to the place in his life where he desires to make Jesus Lord of his life and to receive Him as his Savior. Just now, Father, you've heard him confess his faith in Jesus, and I know that the very angels of heaven are rejoicing over this decision that he's made in his heart. Father, I pray that you will bless Jeff as he follows Jesus in baptism, and then Father, that you will help him all the days of his life to live a faithful life for the cause of Christ; and may many people come to know Jesus as their Lord and Savior because of the decision Jeff has made in his heart this day. In Jesus' name I pray, Amen.

Jeff, that's fantastic! Now, let me ask you, when do you want to be baptized? We can go to the church building right now or would you prefer to walk the aisle on Sunday morning and be baptized at that time? It's entirely up to you.

JEFF: I don't want to wait. Can we go right now?

JOHN: Of course we can. I'm sure there are some people that you want to witness your baptism. Why don't we give them a call right now before we leave for the church.

A BRIEF ANALYSIS

You may be thinking that Jeff was a little too cooperative, that surely leading someone to Christ would never be quite that easy. Yet, the truth is, I've gone through that very presentation hundreds of times where the person to whom I'm witnessing has been every bit that cooperative. There are many people just waiting for someone to help them understand the truth and to urge them to act upon the truth. Notice again how I very simply explained that MAN HAS A PROBLEM — sin; GOD HAS A SOLUTION — the sacrificial death of His Son in payment for man's sin; and MAN MUST RESPOND — accepting God's Son as Savior and Lord by faith.

However, in all honesty, it is also true that many times, presenting the gospel does not go as smoothly as it did in the example I gave. Many people will certainly listen to and even agree with the presentation up to the point of their personal response. It is then that they begin to offer excuses or even ask irrelevant questions. How do you deal with that? That will be the subject of the next chapter.

CHAPTER NINE

DRAWING THE NET

It was Jesus Himself who introduced us to the idea of fishing as an analogy for evangelism. Jesus said to Peter and Andrew while they were casting their fishing nets into the Sea of Galilee, "Follow Me, and I will make you fishers of men" (Matthew 4:19). Most of us who grew up in the church can well remember singing the little chorus, "I Will Make You Fishers of Men," complete with the actions of casting and reeling in our catch. However, first-century fishermen knew nothing of casting rods and reels. Fishing was done with nets that were approximately fifteen feet in diameter and weighted on the edges. They were cast into the sea and then drawn back into the boat with the catch of fish.

We read often in the gospels of the disciples mending their nets, for if there were tears in the cords, the fish would escape. We also read of their washing their nets both in order to preserve them and to maximize their effectiveness. We even read about their casting their nets from the boats into the waters where the best catches were expected. However, mending, cleaning, and casting would have served no purpose if the fishermen had not also drawn the net with its catch back into the boat.

The same thing is certainly true in evangelism. We can be well prepared, learn all the best methods for approaching people, be adept at making a spiritual diagnosis, be effective in guiding a discussion toward spiritual issues, and even more than adequate in presenting the gospel (casting the net). However, if we, or someone, does not draw the net, does not bring that person to a personal commitment of their life to Jesus Christ, then everything else we've done is in vain. Thus the term "Drawing the Net," based on Jesus' fishing analogy, has to do with bringing a person from knowing what they need to do, to actually doing something about it.

Unfortunately, this is where many would-be evangelists fail. Overcoming the fears that often hold people back, they approach the person for whom they are concerned and tell them the truth about Jesus. They explain man's problem, God's solution, and even man's response. But they never get around to asking them to make that response. Or if they do, at the first sign of resistance, they beat a hasty retreat. One thing I've noticed about good fishermen is that they are very patient and persistent. We read on more than one occasion in the gospels of how the disciples fished all night long even though they had no results. But they kept at it and eventually enjoyed an incredible catch (see Luke 5:4-7 and John 21:3-6).

"Drawing the Net" in evangelism means clearly articulating what a person must do and asking them to do it; dealing with the excuses that would delay their decision; and providing them with the proper motivation which would cause them to act. This chapter is designed to provide you with the resources to do those things, but again, the ultimate results are dependent on your actually using these resources.

ASKING THE RIGHT QUESTIONS

Once you have presented the gospel to someone in a clear, concise way, you should always give them the opportunity to decide for Christ right then and there. Never say, "Please think about it," or "I hope you will give your life to Jesus." Encourage that person without further delay to move from intellectual faith, to emotional faith, to volitional faith — from understanding the truth, to wanting to respond to the truth, to responding to the truth.

Do you remember the series of questions with which I closed the gospel presentation in Chapter 8?

> "Don't you really believe in Jesus, that He is the Son of God?" "Don't you really want to be a Christian and live for Christ?" "When the man in the story (the Ethiopian eunuch) came to believe in Jesus, and came to the point in his life that he wanted to accept Jesus as his Lord and Savior, what

did he do next?" "You could make that very decision right here and now. Wouldn't you like to do that this very moment?"

I've used that simple, natural progression hundreds of times with people who have been ready and even anxious to accept Christ. I've often gone into homes during evangelistic crusades where it wasn't even necessary to present the gospel.

I remember such a call in Ohio. It was late in the evening. We had to be at the church building in less than thirty minutes. The preacher told me this young couple had been attending regularly and that several teams of callers had been in their home, but for some reason they had not yet made a decision to accept Christ as Savior and Lord. With hardly any general conversation, I got right to the point. As a matter of fact, we didn't even sit down. "The preacher tells me that you have been regularly attending church and that several folks have already been by to talk to you about becoming Christians. May I ask, do you believe that Jesus Christ is the Son of God, that He died for you on the cross, that He arose again from the grave, and that He wants to be your Savior?" They both answered, "Yes, we do." "Well, don't you really want to be Christians, to accept Jesus as your Lord and Savior, to do what He wants you to do and to be what He wants you to be?" Again they answered in the affirmative. "If you really wanted to, would there be any reason to keep you from becoming Christians today?" "No," they answered. "Would you both like to make such a decision right now?" They looked at each other and smiled, then nodded in the affirmative. I led them in a confession of faith, prayed with them, and then said, "We're going to get out of here so you can get ready for church, for I'm sure you're going to want to publicly confess Christ tonight and be baptized into Him." Again, they didn't hesitate to say that they would be there and do just that.

When I recall such stories, there will be many people reading this book who will say, "It can't be that easy. He's just exaggerating." Certainly every case isn't like that one. There are many people I've never been able to lead to Christ in spite of repeated efforts. But I have had many responses like the one I just mentioned. It is altogether likely that you could too, but you will never know unless you ask.

One of the most effective questions I often use, especially if I sense any hesitation or resistance at all, is, "If you really wanted to, would there be any problem to keep you from becoming a Christian today?" That question will focus your conversation on the real issue that needs to be dealt with, which in most cases is the will of the individual. It also helps them to see that that is the issue. On the other hand, if there are other issues, they will identify them and you can proceed to deal with them.

DEALING WITH EXCUSES

When asked to make a decision, many people will begin to offer excuses as to why they should wait. Remember, an excuse is simply AN ATTEMPT TO DELAY A DECISION. While the person may be sincere, their excuse is often not even legitimate but is instead something they've heard before which Satan offers them as a means of delaying a decision. Don't let excuses cause you to wait. Accept it as a challenge. Realize that this may very well be the last barrier between the person to whom you were witnessing and their salvation.

On one occasion I went to talk to the unsaved husband of one of our church members. I took as my silent partner a fairly new Christian who had never been calling before. I presented the gospel to Bill but when I invited him to accept Christ, rather than saying "Yes," he offered an excuse as to why he should wait. I dealt with his excuse and again asked him to accept Christ. Again, without responding positively or negatively he offered another excuse. I dealt with that one and again asked him to accept Christ. This whole process was repeated over and over. Bill never said, "No," nor did he become upset with my persistence. It was as though he wanted me to convince him (and that often is the case). Finally, he had exhausted his supply of excuses and again I said, "Bill, wouldn't you like to accept Jesus Christ as your Lord and personal Savior this very night?" and he answered, "Yes, I would." We had a great time of rejoicing with his family who had been waiting in another room. We went to the church for a "same hour of the night" baptism. Afterward, my rookie calling partner told me that he had kept count, and that I had asked Bill to accept Christ eighteen times. Yes, but the eighteenth time he said, "Yes!"

Now, what is the best way to deal with an excuse? I've found that it is most effective to simply ask the prospect a question about his excuse. Most people have not logically thought out their excuses. By asking questions you get them to think about what they've said, and more often than not they will destroy their own excuse. Let me illustrate this principle using some of the most common excuses.

"I DON'T KNOW ENOUGH." This may sound like a legitimate excuse at first, but consider the following questions. How much do you think you have to know? Are we saved by knowledge or by faith? Do you believe that you are a sinner? Do you believe that you need a Savior? Do you believe that Jesus Christ is the Son of God and will be your Savior if you accept Him as such? You can go on to show that those are the essentials. There is much more to learn, but it can be more easily and quickly learned as a Christian with the help of the Holy Spirit. A good example to use would be the conversion of the Ethiopian eunuch (Acts 8:26-39); for he knew nothing about Jesus previous to meeting Philip, and he accepted Christ on his first hearing of the gospel.

"I'M NOT GOOD ENOUGH TO BE A CHRISTIAN." It is especially important to deal with this excuse, for it suggests a basic misunderstanding of what it means to become a Christian. You might first ask for clarification, "What do you mean by that? Do you believe anyone is actually good enough?" Next, the misunderstanding itself needs to be challenged. Haven't all of us fallen short? (Romans 3:23). Jesus died for us because we aren't good enough (Romans 5:8, Luke 5:31-32). Salvation is not a matter of what we DO but of what Christ has DONE. A good example is Paul's testimony in

1 Timothy 1:12-15 where he details his past life as the fore-most of sinners, yet glorifies the Lord for His mercy and grace in saving him in spite of his past.

"I'M WAITING FOR A FEELING." The question in response is obvious. What kind of a feeling are you expecting? Does the Lord save us according to our feelings or our faith? You can offer examples of how feeling followed the exercise of obedient faith (Acts 8:39, 16:34). Then you can point out that we are called by the gospel, not a feeling (2 Thessalonians 2:13-15).

"I DON'T THINK I CAN LIVE THE CHRISTIAN LIFE." In response to this sometimes sincere and legitimate excuse you should ask, "Do you believe that God can do what He says He will do?" Then you can lead the prospect to the Scriptures that assure us of God's help in living the Christian life; Scriptures like 1 Corinthians 10:13, 2 Thessalonians 3:3, Philippians 1:6, and Jude 24. Living the Christian life is not a matter of faith in our faithfulness, but faith in Christ's faithfulness.

"I INTEND TO SOMEDAY." The truth is that I've met very few people in America who didn't intend to accept Christ "someday." But the vast majority die lost nonetheless. The question is, "Do you know how long you will live?" You might also ask, "If you knew that this were your last day on earth, would you give your life to Christ today? Do you have any assurance that it is not?" The uncertainty of life should be stressed (James 4:13-17). An excellent example to use is the parable of the Ten Virgins in Matthew 25:1-13. All ten planned to be ready for the coming of the bridegroom, but the five foolish virgins were found unprepared. "Behold, now is the 'acceptable time,' behold now is 'the day of salvation!'" (2 Corinthians 6:2). Other relevant scriptures include Psalm 95:7-9, Proverbs 27:1, Isaiah 55:6, Matthew 24:44, and Acts 22:16.

"THERE ARE SO MANY DIFFERENT CHURCHES, I DON'T KNOW WHAT TO BELIEVE." I can certainly sympathize with people who sincerely voice this reservation. Religious division is a major stumbling block to evangelism. It is no wonder

Christ prayed for the unity of His disciples. But the question is simply this, "Would you agree that however a person became a Christian in the early days of the church as recorded in the Book of Acts would also be the way a person would become a Christian today?" If the answer is yes, then you can simply proceed to study the conversion accounts in the Book of Acts (2:37-41, 8:5-13, 8:26-40, 10:44-48, 16:14-15, 16:25-34, 22:1-16).

"I'M WAITING FOR SOMEONE ELSE." A series of questions is appropriate in response. How long have you been waiting? Has waiting brought either of you closer to a decision? Is there really any reason to believe that continuing to wait will be effective in bringing your friend to Christ? The fact of the matter is that you can lead someone to Christ from your position as a Christian far more effectively than you can urge them to do what you have not done yourself. I have many examples of how a decision by one person resulted in the conversion of the person for whom they were waiting. However, it should be emphasized that salvation is a personal matter, and that a person should give their life to Christ regardless of what anyone or everyone else does.

"THERE ARE TOO MANY HYPOCRITES IN THE CHURCH." The issue here is, are you going to allow the hypocrisy of some to keep you out of heaven itself? If so, you will spend eternity with those very hypocrites, for God, who knows every man's heart, says that the hypocrite is bound for hell (Matthew 23:13-33). However, what we often call hypocrisy is in reality only human weakness. All people, even Christians, sin (1 John 1:8-10). Hypocrisy has to do with the motivation of the heart, and only God is in a position to judge that. Thus Jesus' advice to Peter in John 21:21-22 not to worry about others but to follow Him yourself is certainly relevant to this often-voiced excuse.

"I DON'T THINK I HAVE TO BE BAPTIZED." Because of denominational confusion on the subject of baptism, this often becomes a point of contention. Now, I will never argue the subject of baptism, because baptism is not the issue. If a person is genuinely converted to Christ, then they will do whatever He says. I remember talking to a man in Hutchinson, Kansas many years ago. His hang-up seemed to be on baptism and so I said, "Mr. Jones (not his real name), if the Lord Jesus Himself were to stand here in your living room today and tell you to be baptized, would you do it?" His face grew red with anger; he came up out of the recliner in which he had been sitting and literally screamed, "No sir, I wouldn't do it. I'll go to hell before I'll be baptized!" And unless he repents, that's exactly where he will go; not because he wasn't baptized, but because he never surrendered his heart to Jesus. Baptism, among many other things, is the evidence of a surrendered heart.

Thus when people object to baptism I simply suggest that we look at what the Bible says. I take the person through Matthew 3:13-17, 28:19-20; Mark 16:15-16; Acts 2:38, 8:35-39, 16:30-34, 22:16; Romans 6:3-5; and 1 Peter 3:21. If the mode of baptism is in contention, I might also add John 3:23 and Colossians 2:12. Let the Scriptures convince and convict. If a person's heart is genuinely surrendered to Jesus, they will do what He says when they understand the teaching of His word.

To place baptism in its proper perspective in the plan of salvation, I often use this illustration. When a couple gets married it is not the ceremony that is the essence of their marriage. Indeed, if they do not have love and commitment for each other, then the most beautiful of ceremonies is an empty and meaningless thing. However, if a man and woman do truly love each other and if they have committed their lives to each other, then the ceremony takes on tremendous significance symbolically, legally, affirmationally, and in many other ways. So it is that baptism apart from personal faith in Christ and commitment of one's life to Him means nothing. The only thing it accomplishes is to get you wet. But when there is faith in Christ and a surrender of your life to His will, then baptism takes on tremendous significance to you, to God, and to the world.

THERE ARE CERTAINLY MANY OTHER COMMON EXCUSES with which we have not dealt. To the excuse, "I want to think it over," you can respond with the question, "Specifically, what is it that you need to think over?" The scriptural questions of 1 Kings 18:21 and Acts 22:16 get right to the point. To the idea, "There's too much to give up," you can respond, "Do you believe that a God who loved you so much that He gave His only begotten Son to die for you on the cross would ask you to give up anything that was best for you?" Indeed, Jesus said in John 10:10, "I came that they might have life, and might have it abundantly." And to the suggestion, "God won't send anyone to hell," you can respond, "Do you believe that if man were not headed for hell that God would actually have sent His Son to the cross? Furthermore, God sends no one to hell. He's done His best to keep man out of hell. But if man chooses to reject the Savior then he chooses hell." For every excuse there is a legitimate response.

PROVIDING THE MOTIVATION

You can faithfully present the gospel, ask the right decision questions, answer all the excuses, and the person may even recognize their need to respond; however, if they are not motivated to ACT NOW they may very well delay their decision. It is altogether right and proper that you use various appeals in PERSUADING the prospect to delay no longer.

Few people would argue with the idea that it is RIGHT to become a Christian. But if it is right to accept Christ, then is it not wrong to delay? In reality, becoming a Christian is the MOST RIGHT thing you can ever do.

There is also the appeal for the prospect to consider all the things they are missing by delay. They are missing out on forgiveness, peace, satisfaction, and fellowship. Furthermore, they could miss out on heaven itself if they continue to delay.

Many parents, dads in particular, are moved by the appeal of influence and example. I've talked to a number of men who had no concern for their own salvation, but when I pointed out that they had children following in their footsteps who would very likely reject Christ because of dad, they saw things very differently.

You can also point out that there is the danger in delay of a person's heart becoming hardened and unable to respond to God's grace. The longer you delay becoming a Christian, the more sin you have of which to repent and the less time you have in which to repent. Furthermore, each time you say "No," to Christ there is a hardening process which takes place in which your heart grows calloused. There can come a point of no return which I understand to be the "unpardonable sin" of which Jesus spoke, blasphemy of the Holy Spirit, where you utterly and completely reject His convicting power.

Perhaps the most basic motivation appeal of all has to do with the uncertainty of life, the imminence of the Second Coming, and the reality of judgment. Although I do not try to manipulate people through fear, it is reality that if a person continues to delay giving their life to the Lord, that sooner or later they are going to die or Christ is going to return and they are going to stand before God in judgment UNPREPARED! We should in no way downplay this truth. Quite the opposite, we should emphasize it.

PERSUADING THE LOST

There is no question but what most would-be soul-winners are weakest in this whole area of persuasion. Never fail to ask the person to whom you are witnessing to accept Christ. Don't be afraid to ask them again and again. If they continue to refuse, you can ask to pray with them and for them. Then you can ask them again. However, always leave the door open for a follow-up visit, and maintain the most positive possible attitude.

It was the first day of a revival crusade in the Southwest Missouri town of Phillipsburg, and the preacher and I and our wives were invited to the farm home of Amzi and Lottie Wills for dinner. We had a wonderful meal of real home cooking while carrying on an enjoyable conversation with Amzi and Lottie. The preacher and I excused ourselves and headed out to make some evangelistic calls. It was only after we were well down the road that I learned that Amzi was not a Christian. I insisted that we go back, where I apologized to Amzi for assuming that he was a Christian and proceeded to witness to him about his need for Christ. When we left his home the second time, I was confident that he would be the first one down the aisle that night.

Amzi was present that night and obviously under conviction. However, as the invitation hymn was sung he gripped the back of the pew in front of him and did not come. The same thing happened Monday and Tuesday nights. Wednesday I told the preacher I wanted to go back and see Amzi. It was haying season, and as God would have it we found him taking a break from his work in the fields. I asked him to tell me what was holding him back, and eventually he revealed that he felt that for him to become a Christian would be to condemn his family who had died outside of Christ. As sensitively as possible I reminded him that salvation is a personal thing, and that each one of us must give account of ourselves to the Lord. We had a good visit, and while he did not make a commitment of his life there and then, I honestly felt that he would come to accept Christ that night. However, that night was as before, and so was Thursday night. He would grip the back of the pew until his knuckles would turn white. His face was contorted with an agonizing conviction, but he would not give in to Christ.

It was Friday, the final day of the crusade. I told Carl, the local preacher, that if Amzi did not come to Christ that day I felt he never would. Amzi was already well along in years, and if he came this close to being saved and turned away, the likelihood of his becoming a Christian was virtually nil. I insisted that we go and see him once more, although I had no idea what I could say to him.

When we arrived at his farm, Amzi was in the house drinking a tall glass of iced tea. I can still see him sitting in that platform rocker, across the linoleum-covered floor of their living room. I said, "Amzi, today's the day you are going to give your life to Jesus. As a matter of fact, you are going to go down to the church this afternoon and be baptized into Christ on the basis of your decision to take Him as Savior."

Amzi said, "I don't know, I don't know!" I said, "You do know, Amzi. Lottie, get him a change of clothes (they didn't have baptismal robes), we're going down to the church right now." He said, "I don't know, I don't know." I said, "You do know, Amzi; now, Lottie, go get those clothes."

His wife hardly knew what to do, but she got up at my direction and soon returned with a change of clothes for her husband. I got up and walked across the floor to where Amzi was sitting. I helped him up out of his chair. I walked him across the floor. I put his straw hat on his bald head. I walked him to the car. I helped both him and Lottie into my car. I drove to the church building. I opened the door for Amzi and Lottie. I walked them inside. I seated them on the front pew of the church auditorium. It was then that I said, "Amzi, don't you believe that Jesus Christ is the Son of God and the only Savior of men?" With that, tears flooded his eyes and he answered, "I sure do." "And don't you want to accept him as your Lord and Savior this very day?" The tears were flowing freely now. "Yes, I do," he responded. I led him in a confession of faith and Carl took him back and baptized him. I'll never forget how, when he came up out of the water he said, "We've got to get ole George now." George Cossey was his best friend, and two years later in a return meeting which I preached at Phillipsburg, on the last night, on the last verse of the invitation hymn, Amzi came down the aisle arm-in-arm with George, leading his friend to Christ.

Some might suggest that I went too far, that it was my decision and not his. But extraordinary situations call for extraordinary measures. I had never done what I did with Amzi before nor have I since. But a few years later I was in Springfield, Missouri and heard that Amzi was in St. John's Hospital dying of cancer. I went to see him and hardly recognized him because of the toll the cancer had taken. But he recognized me immediately and began to weep, and tell me how thankful he was that I hadn't given up on him. It was then I knew, that regardless of what anyone else might say, I had done the right thing.

How far can you go in persuading people? When do you

cross the line between what is legitimate and what is not? The answer to those questions is found more in a sensitivity to the Spirit of God than in any hard and fast rules. But this I know, most of us stop far short, too far short, of crossing that line.

CHAPTER TEN

FINDING THE PROSPECTS

It was the first Sunday of a revival meeting in a rural Missouri congregation. I had asked the preacher for his prospect list. He responded, "You're not going to believe this (I knew I wasn't) but there aren't any prospects around here. Everyone is either a Christian or at least a member of some church in the area." I didn't believe him, but neither was I in a position to refute his claim. However, the next morning I climbed into my car and started down the first road I came to, knocking on doors. By noon that day I had located nine families who didn't go to any church anywhere, by making just eleven visits. That week we saw sixteen persons respond to the gospel out of a community that didn't have any prospects.

There is not now, nor has there ever been in the history of the Lord's church, a shortage of prospects. Today there are five billion people living on earth, and only one-third of them make any profession of being Christian. Here in America, a supposedly Christian nation, at least eighty million people are totally unchurched. Obviously, many more are unconverted, but eighty million have no relationship with any church of any kind. However, of those eighty million, 68% believe in the resurrection of Christ; 64% believe Jesus is the Son of God; and 70% say they read the Bible. The prospects are there — good prospects — winnable people. In the midst of such potential, we need to respond like the now-famous Cavalry commander who said, "Men, there are Indians in front of us, Indians behind us, Indians on either side. Charge! And don't let a one of them get away!!!"

In lifestyle evangelism, we will evangelize the people in our sphere of influence. But what of those people with whom we would not ordinarily come in contact? How do we locate and identify those people as prospects that we might in turn carry out a strategy intended to bring them to Christ?

METHODOLOGY

When traveling in crusade evangelism I put together a lot of ideas on the methodology of locating and identifying prospects which were published in the book, *Reaching the Lost Through the Evangelistic Crusade.*[16] Without going into detail here, the list included such ideas as a city-wide or area-wide survey; an inside-the-church survey, in which you list the name of every unsaved or unchurched household member of member households; the use of attendance cards in church services where people indicated their own needs and interest; spiritual concern cards on which you ask members of your congregation to list the names and addresses of people they want to see won to Christ and for whom they are willing to pray daily; new resident lists which can now be purchased from any number of commercial services; Sunday School and Vacation Bible School enrollments; and new convert contacts that you can identify through the use of "I Care" sheets (asking new converts to identify people they want to see won to Christ) which can be a part of your new-member packet.

However, the best prospects are those who come to your building. How can we get them to come? Eighty percent of the members of your church first came because of someone's personal invitation. Therefore, we need to give our people plenty of "excuses" to invite their friends, neighbors, and associates.

The use of SPECIAL DAYS continues to be an effective way of bringing prospects to your services. Over the years we've had dozens of special days, and we're still winning people to Christ that we first contacted through such events years ago. Every year we use Anniversary Sunday as a major push in the fall. When we were much smaller we could sometimes triple our attendance in such an effort. Still today, our attendance swells by hundreds as our people invite their friends to share in our Anniversary Celebration, which is always made more special by well-known musical guests, the testimony of a Christian celebrity, and/or "dinner on the grounds" following the services and provided by the church. We've also used all the major packaged programs such as "Friends Day" and "FRANtastic Days," plus old favorites like Back To Calvary Sunday, Family Reunion Sunday, Guest Sunday, Celebration Sunday, Jubilation Day, God and Country Sunday, and the list goes on and on.

CONCERTS by outstanding Christian artists will not only draw neighboring Christians to your building, but will be another great excuse for your people to invite unsaved friends. Such concerts are not as threatening to the non-Christian as a preaching service. Furthermore, such concerts will get the name of your congregation before the people of the community. At Kingsway we've had every type and every style — from Christian classical to Southern Gospel, from inspirational to Christian rock, from Gospel soul to Gospel country-western. We've had the best of soloists, groups, choirs, and instrumentalists. But in every case we've been able to identify a number of new prospects. We've had special concerts targeting teens. And while there have been many benefits, one of the primary ones has been the addition of many new teen prospects.

NEED-MEETING PROGRAMS not only perform a vital ministry, but also draw new prospects. A special Singles Conference a few years ago nearly doubled our singles ministry involvement immediately. And the met need does not have to be perceived as spiritual. We've sponsored assertive discipline workshops, parenting seminars, safety seminars, CPR classes, seminars for the unemployed, financial counseling, and a host of other need-meeting programs that have appealed to the secular community but have also broken down walls of resistance and allowed us to identify yet more prospects. You have people in your congregation with expertise they could share with the community, and in the process bring prospects into your building.

One of the greatest evangelistic tools and sources of prospects we have is VACATION BIBLE SCHOOL. Now, we don't call it V.B.S. and we don't use a traditional teaching methodology. Our people put an incredible amount of work into it and we invest a great deal of money as well, but it pays off in big dividends evangelistically. Over the years our V.B.S. has taken the form of a Bible Circus, Bible Lands Safari, Race Into Space, Super Friends Adventure Week, A Royal Kingdom Circus, Passport to Adventure, Construction Junction, Treasure Quest, and lots of other fun, innovative themes that allowed us to assemble as many as a thousand kids to teach them about Jesus. And every child has a family. And many of those family members are prospects. Every dollar spent on live elephants and sky-divers; every hour of rehearsal spent preparing for the dramatization of Biblical events; every bit of effort put into the construction of church buildings from around the world for our missions theme or covered wagons for our Western theme — they've all been worth it in terms of families we've contacted and evangelized that we might never have known in a more traditional approach.

PHILOSOPHY

A principle of church growth that bears directly on our subject is that unsaved and unchurched people are most responsive to becoming Christians and responsible church members during periods of TRANSITION. A period of transition is a span of time in which an individual's or family's normal everyday behavior patterns are disrupted by some irregular event that requires an unfamiliar response. Christians need to be mobilized and motivated to assist in bringing Christ's power and the fellowship of the church into such people's lives in a meaningful, long-term way.

For example, immediately following marriage, the couple is very much in a state of transition and open to change. After a divorce, people are in a critical state of transition. The birth of a child, the critical illness of a family member — all of these things frequently cause individuals and families to be open to help and healing from the church. The church must establish systems to identify periods of transition in unchurched people around them, and then reach these people and introduce them to the caring love of Christ and fellowship of the local church. And while speaking of transitions, preachers have got to stay in one place long enough to know and be known and thus provide stability.

What I'm talking about has to do with real needs; and in that regard WE NEED TO BE MORE CONCERNED ABOUT PEOPLE AS PEOPLE than PEOPLE AS PROSPECTS. There is the danger of seeing prospects as objects to be counted rather than people to be loved. Dr. Joe Ellis says that one of the biggest rebukes he ever received was when he took the evangelist to see a certain prospect. "Jim, we just wanted you to know that we're interested in you," he said with a most serious air of feigned concern. Joe was unprepared for his response. "You're not interested in me," shot back the prospect. "The only time you know I'm alive is when you can USE me to meet a goal or achieve success."[17] Have I ever done that, used people? Yes, I have. And so has the church as a whole. That man's words should stand as a stinging rebuke to all of us.

Evangelism must become for all of us a gospel show-and-tell. For evangelism in its Biblical sense is the announcement of the restoration of humanity, of the fallen image redeemed in Christ, the image of God. Evangelism announces the liberating work of God as in Christ He fashions a new humanity. But people want to see that happening; thus the best prospects we locate will be those whose lives we touch through our personal involvement, as they see Christ living in us — serving, ministering, meeting needs.

I see a major task before us being that of developing a genuine sensitivity to the needs of people about us without lowering the communication of the gospel to a mere Madison Avenue philosophy of public relations. We must attune ourselves to the real and perceived needs of people about us. Dietrich Bonhoeffer identifies how we can accomplish that in his book, *Life Together:*

> The first service that one owes to others . . . consists in
> listening to them. . . . Many people are looking for an ear
> that will listen. They do not find it among Christians,

because these Christians are talking when they should be listening. . . . Christians have forgotten that the ministry of listening has been committed to them by Him who is Himself the great listener and whose work they would share. WE SHOULD LISTEN WITH THE EARS OF GOD THAT WE MAY SPEAK THE WORD OF GOD.[18]

Maybe it's time for us to stop asking, "Would you like to come to our church?" and begin going to the unchurched with the sincere statement, "We'd really like to know why you're not going anywhere." At Kingsway we've taken a step in that direction from time to time with a "Care Survey" in which we've simply gone from house to house saying, "We care about people. Do you have needs we can meet, or do you know of people with such needs?" We've left a brochure with a "Care-Line" sticker for their telephone and the invitation to let us know if we can be of help. The most often voiced response has been, "Aren't you going to invite us to your church?" And our response has been, "We'd love to have you come and here are the times of our services, but what we're really here for today is to uncover needs that we can meet."

I'm saying that evangelism must not be seen in isolation from the problems and events that shape the lives of those to whom we proclaim the gospel and before whom we live it. We need to recapture the New Testament lifestyle of those early Christians in whom Christ was living. Martin Luther called them "little Christs," men in whom Jesus Christ was continuing to live His life. They had undergone a fantastic spiritual transformation that revolutionized every aspect of their lives — moral, social, and economic. Jesus Christ touched them with His power and they in turn touched their world with power. They became revolutionaries, Christian style. They touched hypocrisy and turned it into reality. They touched immorality and turned it into purity. They touched slavery and turned it into liberty. They touched cruelty and turned it into charity. They touched snobbery and turned it into equality.

Is it hoping for too much to dream of our having that sort

of impact on the world today? I think not. For the same God who was alive in them is alive in every born-again child of His today. And He is desirous of doing that same work through us. In a world that uses people and loves things, we have the opportunity to show Christ has made a difference in our lives as we love people and use things to meet their needs. When we do, we'll be put in constant contact with all sorts of prospects.

When Jan and I completed ten years of ministry at Kingsway, the congregation put together a celebration which was one of the most memorable of my life. Among the many things they did was to put together a book of letters from friends, acquaintances, associates, and members of the congregation. There were many compliments — some of them highly exaggerated, though I liked to hear them just the same. However, the greatest compliment came from a new family at the time. They wrote it in the form of a prayer. "Through years of Sundays we've listened to preachers who love to preach; but one refreshing Sunday, Lord, we listened to a preacher who loved those to whom he preached. *YOUR* message came through loud and clear." Methodology is important; but it is genuine concern, compassion and love that will make the difference.

CHAPTER ELEVEN

HOW TO BUILD AN EVANGELISTIC CHURCH

The practical insights in this book are gleaned for the most part from the experiences of the Kingsway Christian Church. I am in no way suggesting that our congregation is a model congregation. We certainly haven't arrived, especially in comparison with the church as it was intended to be according to the New Testament. However, the ideas and principles we've shared are not merely theoretical; they have all been tested and found effective in the arena of the local church.

Kingsway Christian Church came into existence in the fall of 1973 with a nucleus of nine families. The group first met in the Avon High School, Avon being an unincorporated area west of Indianapolis. It was and is an area with no real concentration of population, a great deal of open farm land, and seemed to be an unlikely place for building a strong, evangelistic church. However, in that unlikely place God has built such a church.

There are many factors which contribute to the growth of any congregation. If a church is built in the power of God there must be faithfulness to Him and His Word, exaltation of His Son, submission to His Holy Spirit, and preeminence given to the place and practice of prayer. In addition, I believe there are other factors which the Lord has used at Kingsway. I could talk about the importance of music, promotion, organization, warmth and informality. I could write about positive, Biblical preaching; about planning big, or about a philosophy of do it right or don't do it at all. I could mention high leadership expectations, and a hundred other factors. All of these things have contributed to the measure of growth we've experienced. But none of these are the main factor.

The main human factor in building an evangelistic church

is the personal involvement of Christians in leading men and women, boys and girls to Christ. The secret to building an evangelistic church is no secret at all. The more people we involve personally in sharing their faith, the more people we're going to reach for Christ, and the more the church is going to grow. THE WAY TO BUILD AN EVANGELISTIC CHURCH IS TO ENLIST AND INVOLVE EVERY POSSIBLE MEMBER OF THE CHURCH IN CARRYING OUT OUR LORD'S GREAT COMMISSION. In that regard, the early church set a marvelous example (see Acts 5:42, 8:4, 20:20).

There is a verse of Scripture which outlines for us the methodology of building an evangelistic church. As a matter of fact, when followed explicitly, it guarantees success. "He who goes to and fro weeping, carrying his bag of seed, shall indeed come again with a shout of joy, bringing his sheaves with him" (Psalms 126:6).

HE WHO GOES TO AND FRO . . ."

The first step in evangelism is going. The first command in the Great Commission is "GO!" And the main reason we're not winning more people to Christ is because not enough of us are going. It is estimated that 95% of professing Christians never make any specific attempt to win anyone to faith in Christ. The early church, on the other hand, majored in going and therein was found their success.

The Bible is filled with examples of personal soul-winners. Jesus personally dealt with Nicodemus, Zacchaeus and the woman at the well. Andrew brought his brother, Peter, to Christ. Philip led the Ethiopian eunuch to Christ as they rode in a chariot. Paul and Silas led the Philippian jailer and his family to Christ in the middle of the night. Paul attests to the fact in Acts 20:20 that he taught not just publicly but from house to house. The examples go on and on. However, we already recognize the importance of personal evangelism and that it is basic to building an evangelistic church. So let's deal with method.

As a twelve-year-old boy, I was introduced to trotline fishing. My dad, uncle, cousins and I went fishing on a river near

Mountain Grove, Missouri. I was having a wonderful time using my casting rod and reel and had caught a whole stringer full of small bass and crappie. Furthermore, I was the only one who was having any luck. My dad and uncle had hardly caught a thing. That made me all the more upset when they came and took my fish that I had caught and put them on large hooks attached to a long line which they then secured out in the river. Ah, but I understood the next morning when we "ran the trotline" and found we had caught several nice-sized channel catfish.

I've never really cared much for fishing. That trip was one of my few fishing experiences. But I learned a principle that day that can be of tremendous use in the church. The more baited hooks you put in the water, and the better the bait, the more and larger the fish you are going to catch. We have been called to be "fishers of men," and the more approaches we use in trying to win people to Christ, the more we're going to win.

Many churches have only one hook in the water, the Sunday-morning preaching service. If you don't come to accept the Lord on Sunday morning at 11:45 as the congregation sings "Just As I am," then you just don't come. Every preaching service can and should be a "hook" in the water but it is only one. Let's list some others.

A SOUL-WINNING PREACHER — I cannot overemphasize the fact that the preacher must lead the way. The people will not go where he will not lead. Paul's great success in motivating people in the churches to be personal evangelists was his personal example. Preachers should make time to be personally involved in leading the lost to Christ each week. Most of us could win at least someone to Christ every week if we just tried.

SOUL-WINNING ELDERS, DEACONS, & BIBLE SCHOOL TEACHERS — It is my firm conviction that no one has any business in a place of leadership in the church who is disobedient to our Lord's last command and uninvolved in the primary work of the church. For that reason, Kingsway has developed leadership standards which are used in screening potential leaders and which include the standard of personal involvement in the evangelistic program of the church.

CALLING PROGRAMS — No congregation is too small, isolated, or lacking in prospects that it can justify not having specific, organized calling programs to take the gospel to the community. The lost were never commanded to "come to church" but the church is commanded to "go into all the world."

SPECIALIZED MINISTRIES — The church should discover the needs of the community and set about meeting those needs, with the purpose being in part the reaching of those to whom we minister for Christ. With that in mind, our congregation has begun specialized ministries to the deaf and the mentally handicapped. We have a Christian school, two singles ministries, a nursing home ministry, and a benevolence ministry. We have a ministry to the Indiana Girl's School and the Indiana Boy's School. We have a ministry to senior citizens. We minister through sports, drama, multimedia, and music. We have a women's ministry, tape ministry, and a Crisis Pregnancy Center ministry. We have support groups. And of course we have a multifaceted youth program. Every need we meet is just one more "hook" in the water, and our influence for Christ is extended just that much more.

Thus far we've spoken only of ministries related directly to the organized program of the church. What can the individual, concerned Christian do on his own to help build an evangelistic church? First, you can develop a soul-consciousness. Learn to think in terms of whether a person is saved or lost. Develop the habit of inquiring about a person's spiritual condition and using that as an opportunity to witness. Look for opportunities to be with unsaved people in a situation conducive to serious talk. There is "coffee-break evangelism" in which you use your coffee break to speak a word for Christ. Americans drink over 400 million cups of coffee a day. What an opportunity! Then there is "lunch-time evangelism." Take a person to lunch and have an uninterrupted time to share your faith in Christ. How about "social-event evangelism" in which you take an unsaved friend to a class social or include them in social plans with other Christians?

This often breaks down barriers. Several of our present leaders at Kingsway first attended a social event such as our "Sweetheart Classic" ping-pong tournament or our Family Retreat. And of course there is always "public transportation evangelism." When on a bus, plane, or train, you have a captive audience. Use that opportunity to share your faith.

If we are to build great, evangelistic churches, we must get our people involved in sharing their faith. We must make opportunities for them to evangelize through the church program. They must be convicted of the need to witness spontaneously as well. The more people we involve, the more "hooks" we have in the water, the wider our sphere of influence is going to be, and the more unsaved people we're going to reach for Christ. The first step in evangelism and thus in building an evangelistic church is to GO!"

HE WHO GOES TO AND FRO WEEPING . . ."

Going is first; but if we are to be effective, there must also be a compassion, a burden, a concern for the souls of the lost. This is an area in which all of us can be intimately involved, for we need concerned people not only in the pulpit but in the pew, Christians on their knees together. We need Jeremiahs who can weep over the sins of the people. We need more people like the Apostle Paul who said he served the Lord "with tears."

Where are the prayer meetings where we agonize over the lost? How long has it been since you've shed a tear over someone who is headed for hell? Where are the burdened Christians, the people who really care? It is easy to see that as a general rule those who are the most effective in reaching the lost are those who are most concerned.

Once again, I believe the preacher must lead the way. If he is not burdened, it is unlikely that the people will be. If he doesn't weep over the lost, then his people won't. If he doesn't emphasize the fact that Christians are commanded to be evangelists, and he doesn't make heaven and hell real, and he doesn't make much of evangelism as it does take place, then it is unlikely that the congregation is going to have much of a concern or burden for soul-winning. However, every Christian should develop a genuine passion, a burden, a concern for the lost.

"HE WHO GOES TO AND FRO WEEPING, CARRYING HIS BAG OF SEED . . ."

We must go and be concerned, but we must also remember that without planting the seed, the Word of God, there can be no genuine faith and thus no genuine conversion. It is our job to go, weep, and plant the seed; and it is the Holy Spirit's job to bring about conviction and conversion through the word. What a heavy responsibility was lifted from my shoulders when I finally realized I wasn't responsible for converting people. However, I am responsible for going, weeping, and sharing the message.

That message is not one of salvation through good works, ritual or religious affiliation; but of the Son of God, even Jesus, fulfilling the righteous demands of a just God on Calvary's cross. It is the message that all have sinned and need to accept what Christ accomplished for them on that cross. It is a message that men need not suffer hell, for Christ suffered hell on the cross for every man, and that when a person puts his faith or trust in Christ and yields his life in obedience to His Lordship, Christ's righteousness is imputed to him.

Any saved person can tell another person what to do to be saved. However, if we are to build strong, aggressive, evangelistic churches, we must teach and equip our people to effectively share the gospel message. That's why whole chapters have been devoted to training and methodology. But whatever the method, keep the message plain. Stay in the Word! Teach the Word! Love the Word! Spread the Word! The seed is the Word of God.

"SHALL INDEED COME AGAIN WITH A SHOUT OF JOY, BRINGING HIS SHEAVES WITH HIM."

This is God's promise to the man, the woman, the congregation, doing the three aforementioned things. God promises to give the fruit, the rejoicing, to save souls. But that is conditional on our going, weeping, and planting the seed. When we do, God keeps His promises.

I can't save a single soul and neither can you. But we can all go and weep and plant the seed and, praise God, Jesus Christ can save and He will. We can do nothing in and of ourselves, but God can do amazing things with us if we'll claim His promises and yield to His will.

Our topic for this chapter has been, "How To Build An Evangelistic Church." We could have discussed faith and vision, organization, the need to ever be learning, or a number of other important factors. However, the fundamental key in building an evangelistic church is simply that of getting every possible member of the body to be involved in sharing their faith. And may it begin with you and me? Let's go and witness to a lost world. Let's get away from our committee meetings and organizational work, and other well-intentioned activities, and dedicate ourselves to looking for opportunities to share our faith. Let's get out into the highways and hedges and bring the lost to Christ.

CHAPTER TWELVE

TEACHING OTHERS
TO EVANGELIZE

The growth of the church as recorded in the book of Acts is nothing short of fantastic. In Acts 2:41 the church began with 3,000 being saved. In Acts 2:47, "The Lord was adding to their number day by day those who were being saved." In Acts 4:4, "The number of men came to be about 5,000." In Acts 5:14, "All the more believers in the Lord, multitudes of men and women, were constantly added to their number." In Acts 6:1, "The disciples were increasing in number." Within the first century the gospel was preached to the entire Mediterranean world; and this without the benefit of printing press, television, radio, telephone, jet planes, or even automobiles. In a matter of weeks the Jerusalem church filled the entire city with their teaching of Jesus. The high priest said to Peter and John in Acts 5:28, "We gave you strict orders not to continue teaching in this name, and behold YOU HAVE FILLED JERUSALEM WITH YOUR TEACHING and intend to bring this man's blood upon us." It is estimated that in a few months the church in Jerusalem grew to a membership of between fifty and one hundred thousand Christians.

How can such growth be explained? The answer is quite simple. Acts 5:42 holds the key: "And every day, in the temple and from house to house they kept right on teaching and preaching Jesus as the Christ." The secret of the success of the early church was that every follower of Jesus Christ became a soul-winner, a personal evangelist. In Acts 8:1, "A great persecution arose against the church in Jerusalem; and they were scattered throughout the regions of Judea and Samaria, *except the apostles*." Luke continues in vs. 4, "Therefore, those who had been scattered went about preaching the word." It was the norm for those early

Christians to share their faith and in so doing to bring people to Christ.

In 2 Corinthians 5:18 Paul tells us, "All these things are from God, who reconciled us to Himself through Christ, and GAVE US THE MINISTRY OF RECONCILIATION, namely that God was in Christ reconciling the world to Himself, not counting their trespasses against them, and He has COMMITTED TO US THE WORD OF RECONCILIATION. Therefore, WE ARE AMBASSADORS FOR CHRIST, as though God were entreating through us; we beg you on behalf of Christ, be reconciled to God." If that ambassadorship is going to be fulfilled by the modern church, then not only are we going to have to get involved in the ministry of reconciliation personally, but we are going to have to teach others to do so as well. As a matter of fact, we who serve as pastor-teachers in the church have been given that specific responsibility. Paul wrote in Ephesians 4:11-12, "He gave some as apostles, and some as prophets, and some as evangelists, and some as pastors and teachers FOR THE EQUIPPING OF THE SAINTS FOR THE WORK OF SERVICE, to the building up of the body of Christ." Those of us in the ministry may find it easier to do the work ourselves, but to do so is to fail to fulfill the ministry Christ has given us, and is to let multitudes that could be won die and go to hell.

It seems to me there are four basic elements in any program for teaching and involving our people in the practice of personal evangelism. We must first develop in our people a PASSION for the lost. We must make the people aware of the POSSIBILITIES for sharing their faith. There must be PROMOTION or recruitment of the workers. And finally, there must be the actual PREPARATION through teaching and training.

PASSION

If the people in our churches are to have a real passion for the lost, the man in the pulpit must lead the way. If preachers are not burdened for the lost, their people will not be. If preachers do not weep over the lost, their people

won't. If the preacher is not a soul-winner, his people will not
be personal evangelists. Of course, there are exceptions. But
as a general rule, the people will not go where the preacher
will not lead. Paul established great, evangelistic congregations wherever he went. However, he first set the example.
Remember what he said to the Ephesian elders: "You yourselves know, from the first day that I set foot in Asia, how I
was with you the whole time, serving the Lord with all humility and tears and with trials which came upon me through the
plots of the Jews; how I did not shrink from declaring to you
anything that was profitable, and teaching you publicly and
from house to house" (Acts 20:18). It is not enough that I as
a preacher preach and teach evangelism. I must set aside
time on a regular basis to be in people's homes, practicing
what I preach.

However, the message from the pulpit is also very important. Several times a year I preach sermons dealing with
personal involvement in evangelism. And while much of my
preaching is expository, going through books of the Bible, it
is amazing how much of God's Word lends itself to teaching
on evangelism. People need to know that as Christians we are
commanded to be soul-winners. We should teach and preach
that no Christian is obedient to Jesus Christ unless he or she
makes a contribution to the soul-winning program of the
church. One of the first statements Jesus made to His disciples was, "Follow me and I will make you fishers of men"
(Matt. 4:19). To the seventy Jesus said, "The harvest is plentiful, but the laborers are few; therefore beseech the Lord of
the harvest to send out laborers into His harvest. Go your
way; behold, I send you out as lambs in the midst of wolves"
(Luke 10:2-3). We need to emphasize the great commission
as given in Matthew, Mark, Luke, and Acts, and emphasize it
often. Furthermore, a passion for souls is partially dependent
on how real heaven and hell are to the Christian.
Unfortunately, far too many pulpits in this day of "feel good"
preaching are very silent on the reality of what it means to
die without Christ and to be lost eternally.

A burden or passion for souls can also be developed by

stressing what others are doing in the realm of personal evangelism. Often I have had the person who has led another to Christ come with them at invitation time. If not, I always try to mention the person who God has used to bring that person to Christ. And since we often follow the biblical example of baptizing converts immediately, the person who has taught the new disciple is often the one who baptizes them. Nothing I know of gets a person excited about soul-winning more than the privilege of baptizing someone into Christ.

One other thing — we need to emphasize that the lack of a passion or burden for souls does not relieve us of the responsibility. I can assure you that I'm not always anxious to go calling. But I go anyway because Christ commanded it, because people are lost, and because I'm a Christian. And God honors that.

But if we go with a burden, if we go because we are compelled from within, we will certainly be even more effective. The inhabitants of heaven care and are burdened (see Luke 15:7 & 20). In hell men are concerned. Remember the rich man in Luke 16 who said, "I beg you, Father, that you send him to my father's house — for I have five brothers, that he may warn them lest they come to this place of torment" (vss. 27-28). We, too, need to develop in the people we would teach a passion, a burden, a concern for the lost.

POSSIBILITIES

We must also make the people aware of the possibilities for sharing their faith. I believe the most effective way to do so is spontaneously. Therefore, we should cultivate in our people the practice of talking about Jesus to others just as naturally as they might talk about the weather or their favorite ball team. Every day our people come in contact with scores of unsaved people who are potential Christians. Thus we need to teach people to be soul-conscious, to think in terms of whether each person they meet is saved or lost, and to look for opportunities to share their faith.

A preacher in Ohio told me of a man coming to him after a sermon on personal evangelism and asking his advice on how he could possibly be a soul-winner. He had a milk delivery route at night and went to bed about the time everyone else was getting up. The preacher told him he would pray about his dilemma (a favorite delaying tactic of preachers when we don't have an answer) and then he promptly forgot all about it until the next Sunday, when he saw the milk deliveryman approaching. However, it was to inform the preacher of a plan which he had devised on his own. He had written a letter to each of his customers, telling them he was a Christian and that he wanted them to know that he was going to pray for them each night as he made his deliveries. Furthermore, he invited them to leave special prayer requests along with their milk orders.

Soon after leaving the letter with his customers, he noticed that the lights were often on in the middle of the night in one especially affluent home. Then came the prayer request. The mother was very concerned about her teenaged son. He was going through some troubling times and the mother was often up in the middle of the night because of her concern for her boy. The deliveryman not only prayed for the boy, but communicated his concern in notes that he left. Finally the mother asked to talk with him. The eventual outcome was incredible. Not only did the Christian deliveryman offer counsel which helped the parents help their son, but he led the whole family to Christ. His church was in the process of relocation. And the preacher went on to explain that the husband the deliveryman led to Christ was head of one of the largest general contractors in their city. This man personally oversaw the construction of their new multimillion-dollar building and did it at his cost . . . and all because a Christian deliveryman looked for possible ways to share his faith.

Although Kingsway Christian Church is located in Hendricks County some distance west of the city of Indianapolis, we have people who attend from all over the metropolitan area. Why? I wish I could say it was because of the great preaching. But the fact is, they attend because someone from our church family has witnessed to them at work, at school, or through some social or family relationship. They win people to Christ, who in turn come to our church. Eventually many will find church homes closer to where they live. Others will stay where they first came to faith. But the great thing is that everyone can evangelize.

Yes, everyone can do it. You don't have to be smart to evangelize. Some of the most effective soul-winners I've known only had a grade-school education. You don't have to have a good background to be a soul-winner. The adulterous woman at the well led the whole city of Sychar to Christ. You don't have to be polished. Think of Peter — bombastic, impetuous, impulsive — but what a soul-winner he was. You don't have to be physically healthy. I remember a fellow in my college days who was dying of leukemia. But he spent his last days telling people about Jesus. When he was too weak to go to them, he telephoned people from his bed. You don't have to be an adult to be a soul-winner. Many of our teens put our adults to shame in that regard. You don't even have to be a teen. I've known of many people coming to Christ because of the concern of a child.

For that matter, I guess you don't even really have to be a Christian yourself. When we were traveling in evangelistic work my son, Shan, would always quickly make friends with some other child in the local church, usually somewhat older than he. We were in Greenwood, Nebraska. Shan was four years old but had been befriended by nine-year-old Jimmy. I happened to overhear their conversation after services one night. "Jimmy, have you been baptized?" "No, have you?" "No, my dad won't let me; but I would become a Christian if I could." That night on their way home Jimmy said to his mother, "Do you know what Shan Caldwell asked me tonight?" He went on to tell of their conversation and added, "You know, Mom, I really do need to become a Christian." And the next night he came to accept Christ, all because a little child got him to thinking. But we have to show people the POSSIBILITIES for sharing their faith.

Again, if we would all witness spontaneously we could reach our neighbors, our friends, our fellow employees, our schoolmates, the clerk at the supermarket, our barber or beautician, and lots of other folks we constantly come in contact with. But what about all those people we never encounter in the ordinary course of our lives? We also have a responsibility for them. This is where the organized evangelistic program of the church comes into play in providing possibilities for personal evangelism. Furthermore, a person who has gone out in a supervised situation in an organized calling program will find it much easier to witness spontaneously. At Kingsway we have Tuesday night and Wednesday morning adult calling. We have Tuesday night teen calling. We have Bible school and youth coach calling. We have occasional area canvass work as well as occasional periods of intensive decision calling. This is all in addition to shepherding calling by elders and small group leaders. Actually, there is no excuse for any church, regardless of its size or situation, not having a calling program.

There are other possibilities that should not be overlooked. Some of our people lead Bible studies at work and school. Special ministries like Bible clubs, bus ministries, rescue ministries, or ministries to the handicapped offer possibilities for evangelism. There is personal witnessing on busses, trains, and planes. Perhaps you can distribute Christian literature. The possibilities are limitless, but we must make our people aware of those possibilities.

PROMOTION

People must also be personally recruited for training in, and the practice of, evangelism. The best situation in which such recruitment takes place is one in which evangelism permeates the whole program of the church. People will involve themselves in those things they are shown to be most important. Evangelism is not simply to be a department in the church or the responsibility of a committee; it is the main thrust of our entire mission. Preaching, teaching, Bible School, youth groups, music, and building design all relate to evangelism. Our church calendar should also reinforce the importance of evangelism. For instance, nothing preempts evangelistic calling on our church calendar.

But let's get down to some specifics. If you are already involved in personal evangelism, take someone with you when you go to talk to someone about Christ and the church. Encourage other faithful Christians to recruit people to call with them as well. Make evangelistic calling a specific activity on your church calendar, scheduled and emphasized every week. At Kingsway we ask people to make a four-month commitment to our calling programs. It is also helpful to have alternate times for calling, or make available packets of prospect cards through the week for those who can't go at the designated time.

As already has been suggested, make much of those who are soul-winners. Your church will be strong in those areas you brag on most. If you brag on your choir, you'll have a strong choir. People will be excited about that. If you brag on your youth program, it will make people want to be a part of it. The same is certainly true of evangelism. Put evangelism where Jesus put it. It was His first priority. He came "to seek and to save that which was lost."

PREPARATION

Finally, there must be preparation or training provided for those who would be effective evangelists. I honestly believe any saved person can tell another person what to do to be saved. That's certainly what happened in the early days of the church. However, training makes us more confident and more effective. Therefore, the church that will effectively get its people involved in personal evangelism must provide such training.

The best training by far is ON THE JOB TRAINING. We encourage our new converts or inexperienced callers to go with experienced callers. Learning by seeing it done and by participation in the process is better than anything else you can offer. Besides, a new Christian is a tremendous asset to a calling team in the excitement and enthusiasm of their new-found salvation. But whether a new Christian or an old one, if they are new at evangelistic calling, they should know that they won't be sent out without someone experienced to take the lead.

In addition, special evangelism clinics or seminars can and should be held periodically. At Kingsway I sometimes lead them. Other times we have brought in guest leaders. We have also used packaged video programs. The format is never the same. Sometimes we teach evangelism through a Bible school class. It has sometimes been a five-night seminar or a Friday night and all-day Saturday seminar. Other times we've offered training on a certain week night for several successive weeks. The possibilities are numerous and the resources even more so. We also train one-on-one as well as in small groups. The chapters on "Making a Call," "Presenting the Gospel," and "Drawing the Net" would all be appropriate resources to use in such training.

What I'm trying to say is well illustrated in an incident that took place in a hotel lobby in Chicago some time ago. A Christian man walked toward a couple sitting in the lobby. Just as he approached, the man got up and walked away but the Christian continued and approached the lady. After greeting her, he asked, "Are you a Christian?" She wasn't. But God had already been dealing with her heart, and as the Christian man witnessed to her she began to weep. When her husband returned from his trip to the newsstand, he asked why she had been crying. She told him of the conversation she had had with the Christian. Her husband was angry. "Why didn't you tell him to mind his own business?" he asked. "Because," she answered, "he talked to me like it was his business."

Christians, we must communicate to one another that evangelism, soul-winning, reaching the lost, witnessing for Christ — IS OUR BUSINESS. The Lord has told us it is our business. And we must recruit, train, teach, and encourage as many others as possible to evangelize with us.

CHAPTER THIRTEEN

FULFILLING OUR MANDATE

I was 13 years old and a bit of a runt. Dad had a business in Springfield, Missouri, but he also operated a farm several miles north of town. It was hay season and a nice crop of alfalfa had been cut, dried, raked and baled. However, heavy rains were moving in and all that hay could be damaged, if not ruined, if it wasn't gathered from the fields and put into the barn. BUT THERE WAS A PROBLEM. There were no hayhands available. Everyone was doing something else. And so a 13-year-old runt and one big farmboy in his late teens or early twenties were sent to do what ordinarily would have taken a crew of six or eight.

Fortunately, the truck had a side loader. So I drove, the loader picked up the bales, and my buddy stacked them on the truck. Then I drove the truck to the barn where he threw the bales on the hay elevator. I pulled them off in the loft, dragged them across the floor, and stacked them at the far end. We worked without rest from early morning until late that evening when the rains finally hit. Fortunately we got most of the hay in. Only a few bales were damaged or ruined. But no hay needed to have been lost. Furthermore, I remember being sick in bed for two days; and it was all because of a lack of workers.

Jesus said that what was true that day physically has always been true spiritually. The problem has never been with the harvest, but with the reapers. Men are lost, but they can be saved. Hearts are hard, but they can be penetrated by the gospel. Sinners are blinded, but Christ can open blinded eyes. Sinners are enslaved, but Christ releases captives. The lost are spiritually dead, but Jesus specializes in raising the dead. The basic facts about sinful men have never changed, but neither have the basic facts about the power of the gospel. Around the world, in all ages and all lands, the harvest has been plentiful but the laborers have been few. Furthermore, the harvest is more plentiful than ever before today.

From country to country and even from community to community, there will be differing levels of receptivity to the gospel. There will be times of sowing and then times of reaping, times of greater opportunity and times of lesser opportunity. But all around the world, multitudes of people are ripe for the gospel and could be won by Spirit-filled, impassioned and zealous workers. THE PROBLEM IS NOT WITH THE HARVEST BUT WITH THE LIMITED WORKFORCE — not with sinners as much as with saints. As we come to the close of this book, I want to focus on this problem; consider the potential; and once again underscore the priority of the harvest.

THE PROBLEM

On three different occasions, Jesus identified the problem as a lack of workers for the harvest. We read in Matthew 9:36-38,

> And seeing the multitudes, He felt compassion for them, because they were distressed and downcast like sheep without a shepherd. Then He said to His disciples, "The harvest is plentiful, but the workers are few. Therefore beseech the Lord of the harvest to send out workers into His harvest."

His tender heart moved with compassion, I believe His voice trembled and there were tears in His eyes when He pleaded with the disciples to pray for laborers.

On another occasion, Jesus was going through Samaria. He had that well-known encounter with the woman at the well of Sychar. While she ran off to town to tell the people that she had found the Messiah, Jesus said to His disciples, "Do you not say, 'There are yet four months, and then comes the harvest'? Behold, I say to you, lift up your eyes, and look on the fields, that they are white for harvest" (John 4:35). The

144

disciples didn't recognize that even here in this Samaritan village, with its rejected and despised inhabitants, there was a great harvest just waiting to be gathered. Physically it was still four months before harvest time in Palestine, and a spiritual harvest seemed even further removed. Actually, the disciples were so concerned with their own physical hunger that they didn't stop to consider the spiritual needs of the people anyway. But Jesus said, "Lift up your eyes, and look on the fields, that they are white for harvest." And in proof of what He spoke, that one woman who came to know Christ as the Messiah brought the entire town out to meet Him, and verse 39 tells us that "many of the Samaritans believed in Him because of the word of the woman who testified, 'He told me all the things that I have done.'" How ripe was the harvest.

Then there was the time Jesus called seventy disciples, in addition to the twelve, and He told them the same thing. "Now after this the Lord appointed seventy others, and sent them two and two ahead of Him to every city and place where He Himself was going to come. And He was saying to them, 'The harvest is plentiful, but the laborers are few; therefore beseech the Lord of the harvest to send out laborers into His harvest'" (Luke 10:1-2). The fields were just as white and wasting among the Jews as among the Samaritans. And although the seventy may have had little training or experience, Jesus sent them forth because the need was so great. You see, Jesus can use anyone who is willing — even the inexperienced, the untrained, and workers with only ordinary abilities. Availability has always been more important than ability.

The problem in Samaria and Judea was the problem that has plagued the work of the Lord all these years around the world. It is as true in America as it was in Samaria and Judea; and it is as true in 1995 as it was in 32 A.D. There are souls to be won. There are hearts that are hungry. There are fields that are white. But there are not enough people who care enough to win souls. The problem was not with the harvest then, nor is it now. The problem was, and is, with the laborers.

Several years ago in Kansas City, Missouri, a 6-year-old boy named Timothy Adams got to playing on his way home from kindergarten and simply forgot to go home. When he was ninety minutes late, his mother called the police. Suddenly there was a booming, thundering voice in the heavens: "Timothy Adams, go home! Timothy Adams, go home!" Within minutes, policemen William Dycus and James Treece, in a police helicopter, saw a boy streaking for home. A few minutes later Mrs. Adams called the police again to report the safe arrival of her 6-year-old son who had run into the house, wide-eyed and excited, and announced, "A big voice in the sky just told me to come home." Mrs. Adams said she never said anything to clear up the mystery for him.

Now, Timmy hadn't meant to be bad. He had just gotten involved with other things. And the same thing is true of so many Christians. They don't set out to disobey God. They just get caught up in other things and forget all about the crop we are called to reap. The church in the closing years of this twentieth century desperately needs to hear God's big voice in the sky commanding us all to go work in His harvest.

THE POTENTIAL

Jesus made it clear that the plentiful harvest of which He spoke would continue to the end of the age. The potential harvest is greater than ever, and a faithful reading of the Bible will reveal that successful evangelism on an unlimited scale is possible today, depending primarily on the reapers. Sinners are the same in all ages. God is the same in all ages. And the gospel is the same in all ages. To say that changing times make it harder to win souls is an idea not even hinted at in Scripture. Indeed, it may be nothing more nor less than a cop-out for many who are not willing to pay the price.

Consider these Biblical promises. There is the soul-winning promise of Psalm 126:6, "He who goes to and fro weeping, carrying his bag of seed, shall indeed come again with a shout of joy, bringing his sheaves with him." God has never set aside that promise. Then there is the law of sowing and reaping in Galatians 6:7-8, "Do not be deceived, God is not mocked; for whatever a man sows, this he will also reap. For the one who sows to his own flesh shall from the flesh reap corruption, but the one who sows to the Spirit shall from the Spirit reap everlasting life." The law of cause and effect, of action and reaction, is still in effect. Those who sow will bring back a harvest in direct proportion to their sowing.

In 2 Peter 3:9 we read, "The Lord is not slow about His promise, as some count slowness, but is patient toward you, not wishing for any to perish but for all to come to repentance." God loves sinners. God wants them saved. And God has not changed His plans. Let's be honest: sometimes the fire in our hearts burns low, our compassion may be dulled, and many churches have lost their fire and vision. But the fire has not burned low in the heart of Christ. His love is not dulled. He has not given up. And He is not willing that any should perish but that all should come to repentance. It is a central tenet of Scripture that evangelism is the primary purpose of the church throughout the ages, and the winning of the multitudes is the desire of the Lord Jesus.

Furthermore, the potential only increases. At the end of the first century the world's population was 250 million. In 1000 A.D. it had increased to 450 million. By 1500 A.D. it was 545 million. It was not until 1830 that one billion people lived on the earth at the same time. One hundred years later it was two billion, and by the end of this decade there will be between six and seven billion people living here, with seventy percent in Asia, Africa, and Latin America. The world's population increases by 70 million a year, 192,000 per day, or 8,000 per hour. India alone is adding 13 million people each year. Now, we can let such numbers intimidate and discourage us, or we can see the incredible potential and be motivated to get on with the job of fulfilling our mission.

The harvest is plentiful! It will be plentiful to the end of the age. The problem always has been and is now a lack of laborers. The trouble is not with the wickedness of the world. No, the trouble is with the workers for the harvest. There is no shortage of potential.

Actually, I am seeing signs that that tremendous potential

is being tapped. On a recent trip to Myanmar (Burma), I found that in spite of government opposition and Buddhist cultural oppression, churches are flourishing. There are a number of congregations running over 1,000 in attendance, and several over 2,000. While in Southeast Asia I saw, first-hand, doors opening where they had previously been closed. Even as I am writing, Kingsway missionaries Fred and Amanda Abel are preparing to move to Phnom Penh, Cambodia to go through such an open door. In India our missionaries P.V. and Molly John are now reaching whole people groups such as the Lombardies, previously untouched by the gospel. In Kenya I was so impressed with the work of the Christian Missionary Fellowship missionaries among the Masai tribal people, although often at great personal sacrifice. And right here in central Indiana many Bible-preaching churches are having unprecedented success in reaching out to the lost. Doors of opportunity are opening all over the world and laborers are going through them. Not enough are going. But more are going. More and more people are making the fulfillment of the Great Commission a priority in their lives.

THE PRIORITY

I know I've already devoted a great deal of attention in this book to the priority of evangelism. However, unless we understand that and are motivated to do something about it, everything else I've written will be in vain. So before I close, I want to list for you ten reasons why being laborers in the harvest, fulfilling the primary mission of the church, must continue to be our priority.

1. TO FULFILL THE MISSION OF JESUS — That's why He came to seek and to save the lost.
2. TO OBEY GOD'S COMMAND — "Go therefore and make disciples of all nations" is repeated in one way or another again and again in Scripture.
3. TO KEEP SINNERS FROM PERISHING — "For God so loved the world, that He gave His only begotten Son, that whoever believes in Him should not PERISH, but

have eternal life." Perish . . . lost . . . condemned to a Christless hell for all eternity . . . the very thought should motivate us to keep evangelism our priority.

4. TO INCREASE THE JOY OF HEAVEN — "There is joy in the presence of the angels of God over one sinner who repents" (Luke 15:10).

5. TO RESPOND TO THE PLEA OF HELL — The haunting words of Luke 16:27-28 should motivate us as the rich man in hell pleaded, "I beg you, Father, that you send him to my father's house — for I have five brothers — that he may warn them, lest they also come to this place of torment."

6. TO MEET OUR RESPONSIBILITY — Remember the words of Paul, "I am under obligation both to Greeks and to barbarians, both to wise and to the foolish" (Romans 1:14). We are responsible for the lost. We are our brother's keeper.

7. TO EXPERIENCE PERSONAL JOY AND FULFILLMENT — Again, the promise of Psalm 126:6 is that if we will go with a heart of compassion and sow the seed of the Word of God, that we will indeed experience the joy of harvest.

8. TO DEMONSTRATE GODLY WISDOM — Proverbs 11:30 says, "He who is wise wins souls."

9. TO MEET THE CHALLENGE OF TIME — Romans 13:11-12 reminds us of the time, "That it is already the hour for you to awaken from sleep. The night is almost gone, and the day is at hand." Or returning to the analogy of the harvest, one of the saddest verses in the Bible is Jeremiah 8:20, "Harvest is past, summer is ended, and we are not saved."

10. We must make being laborers in the harvest a priority TO RESPOND TO THE PRAYER BURDEN OF OUR LORD. "Beseech the lord of the harvest to send out workers into His harvest" (Matthew 9:38).

While in Yangon (Rangoon) I stayed at a small guest house that often houses preachers, missionaries, and Christian workers. The owner's daughter, Thit Thit, a very intelligent college student in her early twenties, was our housegirl. She spoke fluent English. Late one evening I was sitting in the living room reading. She was doing her homework at a table nearby. Fred Abel had given her a New Testament and it was lying on the table. "Thit Thit," I asked, "have you ever read the New Testament?" "No, I haven't," she replied. "Well, has anyone ever told you about Jesus?" Again her answer was "No." Please remember, this is an inn where missionaries stay frequently and preachers come and go. Yet no one who had flown thousands of miles to preach had ever told this sweet Buddhist girl about Jesus. She told me that she had seen the Jesus movie and another movie, which I finally figured out to be *The Ten Commandments*. That was the sum total of her knowledge of the Bible. So I began to tell her of Jesus.

"Dr. John, may I ask you a question?" "Of course, Thit Thit." "In the movie they killed Jesus by nailing Him to a cross. Why did they do that?" What an incredible question — why indeed? For the biggest part of the next hour I presented the gospel to someone even less knowledgeable than the Ethiopian eunuch. She hung on my every word. I wish I could tell you that she accepted Christ that evening. She did not, although I'm very hopeful that she will if she has not already. But my point is, they are there, all around us. There are people who are ready for harvest — open, receptive, responsive. We dare not pass them by! And they live right down the street from you.

It has always seemed the epitome of hypocrisy for people in America to send money to India to witness to a Hindu while not speaking to their next-door neighbor about Jesus. But even those of us who do go have sometimes missed those who stand right at our front door. We need to begin wherever we are and GO FROM HERE!

I remember it well. The year was 1967 and it was the coldest day on which a professional football game was ever played. In a 67-below-zero chill factor, the Green Bay Packers entertained the Dallas Cowboys for the division championship. With less than a minute to go the Packers, trailing by just two points, pushed the ball to Dallas' two-yard line. As one, the tens of thousands of Packer fans who had endured the frigid cold stood to their feet and began to cheer, "GO! GO! GO!" Sportscasters reported it being the most electrifying, pulsating, crowd noise they had ever heard — reverberating, throbbing through the stands, charging the souls of the players, pumping their adrenaline level to the skies. The quarterback called the signal, and the center hiked the ball. As one man the indomitable Packers, driven by the cheers of their fans, pushed the ball across the goal line for the winning touchdown.

History has recorded the familiar sayings of her sons. Who can forget Patrick Henry's "Give me liberty or give me death," or MacArthur's "I shall return"? But nothing in or out of sacred literature can compare with our Lord's last command, "Go into all the world and preach the gospel to every creature."

We stand at our greatest hour of opportunity. We are at the final juncture of world history. Kingdoms crumble and men's hearts fail them for fear. But what an hour this is for the church and the cause of worldwide evangelism! With knees bent in prayer and with hearts devoted to the task, may this be our finest hour as we seize the moment of opportunity. Surely the Father, the Son, and the Holy Spirit, as well as the redeemed of the ages, the saints of the Old Testament, the New Testament, and all church history — are straining at the precipice of heaven saying, "GO! GO! GO!" Go into all the world! Go, for the harvest is plentiful but the workers are few. Go, fulfill the mission, preach the message and then obey the mandate you have been given. And do it NOW!

NOTES

Chapter 1

1. Howard J. Clinebell, Jr., *Basic Types of Pastoral Counseling*, (Nashville: Abingdon, 1966), pp. 13-14.
2. C.H. Dodd, *The Apostolic Preaching and Its Development*, (New York: Harper & Brothers, 1954).

Chapter 2

3. Robert L. Sumner, *Biblical Evangelism In Action*, (Murfreesboro, TN: Sword of the Lord, 1966), p. 228.

Chapter 3

4. Tim Stafford, "EVANGELISM: The New Wave Is a Tidal Wave." *Christianity Today*, 18 May, 1984, p. 65.

Chapter 4

5. James F. Engel, "Who's Really Doing Evangelism?" *Christianity Today*, 16 December 1991, pp. 35-37.
6. *The Indianapolis Star*, 3 December 1994, p. 05.

Chapter 5

7. James F. Engel, *Contemporary Christian Communications*, (Nashville: Thomas Nelson, 1979), pp. 68-69.
8. James F. Engel & Wilbert Norton, *What's Gone Wrong With the Harvest?* (Grand Rapids: Zondervan, 1975) p. 45.
9. Joseph Aldrich, *Lifestyle Evangelism*, (Portland: Multnomah, 1981), p. 94.
10. Engel, *Contemporary Christian Communications*, pp. 121-122.

Chapter 6

11. Bill Hybels & Mark Mittleberg, *Becoming a Contagious Christian*, (Grand Rapids: Zondervan, 1994), pp. 123-131.
12. W. Oscar Thompson, Jr., *Concentric Circles of Concern*, (Nashville: Broadman, 1981), p. 21.
13. Bill Bright, *Witnessing Without Fear*, (San Bernardino, CA: Here's Life, 1987), p. 89.
14. Ibid., pp. 95-101.

Chapter 7

15. Marshall Shilley, "Home Visitation: How Well Does It Work?" *Leadership*, Spring, 1984, pp. 79-83.

Chapter 10

16. John Caldwell, *Reaching the Lost Through the Evangelistic Crusade*, (Joplin, MO: College Press, 1977), pp. 17-22.
17. Joe Ellis, class notes, "The Effective American Congregation," Cincinnati Bible Seminary, 1983.
18. Dietrich Bonhoeffer, *Life Together*, trans. John W. Doberstern (New York: Harper & Row, 1954), p. 97

BIBLIOGRAPHY

Aldrich, Joseph. *Life-Style Evangelism*. Portland, OR: Multnomah, 1981.

Arn, Win & Charles Arn. *The Master's Plan*. Pasadena, CA: Church Growth Press, 1982.

Autrey, C.E. *Basic Evangelism*. Grand Rapids: Zondervan, 1959.

Bisagno, John R. *How To Build An Evangelistic Church*. Nashville: Broadman, 1971.

_____. *The Power of Positive Evangelism*. Nashville: Broadman, 1968.

Bright, Bill. *Tell It Often – Tell It Well*. San Bernardino, CA: Here's Life Publishers, Inc.

_____. *Witnessing Without Fear*. Nashville: Nelson, 1993.

Caldwell, John. *Intimacy With God*. Joplin: College Press, 1991.

Calver, Clive; Derek Copley; Bob Moffet; Jim Smith. *A Guide To Evangelism*. Hants, UK: Marshall Morgan & Scott, 1984.

Campolo, Tony & Gordon Aeschliman. *50 Ways You Can Share Faith*. Downers Grove, IL: InterVarsity, 1992.

Chafer, Lewis Sperry. *True Evangelism*. Grand Rapids: Zondervan, 1919.

Coleman, Robert E. *Evangelism In Perspective*. Harrisburg, PA: Christian Publications, Inc., 1975.

_____. *The Master Plan of Evangelism*. Old Tappan, NJ: Revell, 1963.

Crane, Charles. *A Practical Guide To Soul-Winning*. Joplin: College Press, 1987.

Edwards, Gene. *How To Have A Soul-Winning Church*. Montrose, CA: Soul Winning Publications, 1963.

Eisenman, Tom L. *Everyday Evangelism*. Downers Grove, IL: InterVarsity, 1987.

Ellis, Joe. *The Personal Evangelist*. Cincinnati: Standard, 1964.

Engel, James F. *Contemporary Christian Communications*. Nashville: Nelson, 1979.

Engel, James F. & Norton, Wilbert. *What's Gone Wrong With The Harvest?* Grand Rapids: Zondervan, 1975.

Falwell, Jerry. *Capturing A Town For Christ.* Old Tappan, NJ: Revell, 1973.

Ford, Leighton. *Good News Is For Sharing.* Elgin, IL: Cook, 1977.

Forder, Reg A. *Soul-Winning.* Englewood Cliffs, NJ: Prentice-Hall, 1984.

Gatewood, Otis. *You Can Do Personal Work.* Nashville: Williams Printing Co., 1956.

Green, Michael. *Evangelism In The Early Church.* Grand Rapids: Eerdmans, 1970.

_____. *Evangelism Now and Then.* Downers Grove, IL: InterVarsity, 1979.

_____. *Evangelism Through The Local Church.* Nashville: Nelson, 1992.

_____. *First Things Last.* Nashville: Discipleship Resources, 1979.

Hale, J. Russell. *The Unchurched.* New York: Harper & Row, 1980.

Hawkins, O.S. *Drawing The Net.* Nashville: Broadman, 1993.

Hendee, John. *Smart Fishing.* Cincinnati: Standard, 1991.

Hunter, George G. III. *The Contagious Congregation: Frontiers In Evangelism and Church Growth.* Nashville: Abingdon, 1979.

Huston, Sterling W. *Crusade Evangelism And The Local Church.* Minneapolis: World Wide Publications, 1984.

Hybels, Bill & Mark Mittelberg. Becoming A Contagious Christian. Grand Rapids: Zondervan, 1994.

Kennedy, D. James. *Evangelism Explosion.* Wheaton, IL: Tyndale House, 1983.

Korthals, Richard G. *Agape Evangelism: Roots That Reach Out.* Wheaton, IL: Tyndale House, 1980.

Leavell, Roland Q. *Evangelism: Christ's Imperative Commission.* Nashville: Broadman, 1979.

Lewis, Larry L. *Organize To Evangelize.* Nashville: Broadman, 1988.

Little, Paul E. *How To Give Away Your Faith.* Downers Grove, IL: InterVarsity, 1966.

Lockyer, Herbert. *The Art Of Winning Souls.* Grand Rapids: Zondervan, 1954.

McPhee, Arthur G. *Friendship Evangelism.* Grand Rapids: Zondervan, 1978.

Malone, Tom. *Essentials Of Evangelism*. Murfreesboro, TN: Sword Of The Lord Publishers, 1958.

Moyer, Larry & Cam Abell. *142 Evangelism Ideas For Your Church*. Grand Rapids: Baker, 1990.

Packer, J.I. *Evangelism & The Sovereignty Of God*. Downers Grove, IL: InterVarsity, 1961.

Pannell, William. *Evangelism From The Bottom Up*. Grand Rapids: Zondervan, 1992.

Posterski, Donald C. *Reinventing Evangelism*. Downers Grove, IL: InterVarsity, 1989.

Prince, Matthew. *Winning Through Caring*. Grand Rapids: Baker, 1981.

Rand, Ron. *Won By One*. Ventura, CA: GL Publications, 1988.

Rowlison, Bruce. *Creative Hospitality*. Campbell, CA: Green Leaf Press, 1981.

Sisson, Dick. *Evangelism Encounter*. Wheaton, IL: Scripture Press Publications, Inc., 1988.

Stephen Ministries. *Caring Evangelism: How To Live And Share Christ's Love*. St. Louis: Stephen Ministries, 1992.

Stott, John R. W. *Christian Mission In The Modern World*. Downers Grove, IL: InterVarsity, 1975.

_____. *Our Guilty Silence*. Grand Rapids: Eerdmans, 1967.

Streett, R. Alan. *The Effective Invitation*. Old Tappan, NJ: Revell, 1984.

Sumner, Robert L. *Biblical Evangelism In Action*. Murfreesboro, TN: Sword Of The Lord Publishers, 1966.

Sweeting, George. *The No-Guilt Guide To Witnessing*. Wheaton, IL: Scripture Press, 1991.

Thompson, Jr., W. Oscar. *Concentric Circles Of Concern*. Nashville: Broadman, 1981.

Wagner, C. Peter. *Church Growth And The Whole Gospel*. New York: Harper & Row, 1981.

Wardle, Terry. *One To One*. Camp Hill, PA: Christian Publications, 1989.

Worrell, George E. *How To Take The Worry Out Of Witnessing*. Nashville: Broadman, 1976.